The
Gift

of Eternal Life

The Gift

of Eternal Life

*Favorite Writings on Our Divine Origin,
Mortal Purpose, and Eternal Destiny*

DESERET BOOK

SALT LAKE CITY, UTAH

Cover illustration: *He Is Risen* © Greg Olsen

Visit us at deseretbook.com

Library of Congress Cataloging-in-Publication Data

The gift of eternal life : favorite writings on our divine origin, mortal
purpose, and eternal destiny.
    p.   cm.
  Includes bibliographical references.
  ISBN 1-57008-908-6 (alk. paper)
  1. Pre-existence.   2. Future life—Church of Jesus Christ of
Latter-day Saints.   3. Church of Jesus Christ of Latter-day Saints—
Doctrines.   I. Deseret Book Company.   II. Title.

BX8643.P67G54 2003
236'.2—dc21   2003000780

Printed in the United States of America   18961-7030
R. R. Donnelley and Sons, Crawfordsville, IN

10   9   8   7   6   5   4   3   2   1

Contents

Our Beginnings in Glory

Falling to Mortality

Priorities, Perspectives, and Promises

The Doorway of Death

An Eternity of Glory

Thanks to the following, whose efforts
helped make this book possible:

Director of Publishing, Deseret Book Company
Cory H. Maxwell

Assistant Director of Publishing
Jana S. Erickson

Compiler and Editor
Jay A. Parry

Editorial Assistant
Lisa Mangum

Research Assistant
Dee Ann Earl Barrowes

Art Director
Thomas E. Hewitson

Cover Art
Greg Olsen

Typography
Kent R. Minson

Proofreaders
Amy Felix
Chris Graham
Ruth Howard

Permissions
Jan Jensen

And special thanks to the authors from many generations whose inspired
and eloquent words have blessed us with increased understanding and gratitude for God's incomparable gift of eternal life.

Our Beginnings in Glory

Where wast thou when I laid the foundations

of the earth? . . . When the morning stars sang

together, and all the sons of God shouted for joy?

JOB 38:4, 7

"Go and Be Faithful"

John Taylor

Whence comest thou? . . . Knowest thou not that eternities ago thy spirit, pure and holy, dwelt in thy Heavenly Father's bosom and in his presence, and with thy Mother, . . . surrounded by thy brother and sister spirits in the spirit world, among the gods? That as thy spirit beheld the scenes transpiring there, and thou grewest in intelligence, thou sawest worlds upon worlds organized and peopled with kindred spirits who took upon them tabernacles, died, were resurrected, and received their exaltation on the redeemed worlds they once dwelt upon. Thou [wast] willing and anxious to imitate them, waiting and desirous to obtain a body, a resurrection, and exaltation also. . . .

At length the time arrived, and thou heard the voice of thy Father saying, go . . . to yonder lower world, and take upon thee a tabernacle, and work out thy probation with fear and trembling, and rise to exaltation. But . . . remember you go on this condition, that is, you are to forget all things you ever saw, or knew to be transacted in the spirit world; . . . you must go and become one of the most helpless of all beings that I have created, while in your infancy; subject to sickness, pain, tears, mourning, sorrow, and death. But when truth shall touch the cords of your heart, they will vibrate; then intelligence shall illuminate your mind, and shed its lustre in your soul, and you shall begin to understand the things you once knew. . . . Go and be faithful as thou hast been in thy first estate.

Spirit Children of God

Bruce R. McConkie

All men are spirit children of God the Eternal Father. In the premortal life, we all dwelt in his presence, saw his face, and heard his voice. We were as well acquainted with him in that day as we are with our earthly fathers in this. The spirit within us is the offspring of God. Now housed in a tabernacle of clay, it is the intelligent, sentient, believing, knowing part of the human personality. The mind of man is in the spirit.

The probationary nature of our mortal estate calls for us to forget the life we lived and the experiences we had when we dwelt in the courts of the Eternal King. But it does not divest us of the spiritual and mental talents we acquired while in that eternal world. We are born into mortality with every innate capacity, every instinct to believe truth and cleave unto light, every faculty and ability with which we were then endowed.

Immortal, Individual Spirits

Robert J. Matthews

Human beings are individual, intelligent, thinking, accountable spirit personages. Some spirits are female; others are male. Spirits are capable of love, hate, joy, sorrow, obedience, disobedience, loyalty, rebellion, and many other character traits and attributes. Spirits are immortal; they never die. They were begotten by our heavenly parents.

The human spirit is a personage that resembles the physical body. Spirit substance is real matter but is considerably more refined than the physical substance of the mortal, fallen, temporal world of earth life. . . .

Of the nature of spirits the Prophet Joseph Smith has written that "the spirit is a substance; that it is material, but that it is more pure, elastic and refined matter than the body; that it existed before the body, can exist in the body; and will exist separate from the body, when the body will be mouldering in the dust; and will in the resurrection, be again united with it" (*Teachings of the Prophet Joseph Smith*, 207). . . .

There is a great variety of intelligence and capacity among spirits. Since all spirits had agency in premortality, variety and gradation soon became apparent. Some spirits became noble and great in knowledge and in character. Likewise, some did not. The greatest of all, of course, is he whom we know as Jehovah, or later as Jesus Christ.

Chosen by the Divine

Truman G. Madsen

There is in all of us an apparently infinite, and certainly ultimate, need for a rich, abiding, undergirding, trustworthy love. This is a love that reaches in and through the self, outward to others, and upward to the highest in the universe. In the ordinary world, even the world of religion, this craving finds extremely rare fulfillment, though it is talked about ceaselessly. But a dawning understanding is the key to its creative source and the beginning of its increase and transformation: that man was known and loved profoundly even prior to mortal birth; that love, indeed, drew him and his Eternal Father together in a sphere of perfected light and glory; that he, distinct from all other beings, animate or inanimate, in the universe, is a chosen and begotten spirit of the Divine; that this sonship, as well as the "second birth" through Jesus Christ, is at the core of any question about the meaning of life.

Of this sweeping awareness, the Prophet Joseph spoke to a multitude of twenty thousand enthralled under his voice:

"This is good doctrine. It tastes good. I can taste the principles of eternal life, and so can you. They are given to me by the revelations of Jesus Christ. . . . and when I tell you of these things which were given me by inspiration of the Holy Spirit, you are bound to receive them as sweet, and rejoice more and more" (*Teachings of the Prophet Joseph Smith*, 355).

Man has always believed that somehow God could be in

his heart. Now he realizes that godliness is veritably engrained in him through a divine lineage. And the whole of his soul lights up.

A child orphaned and cuffed about in a hostile world craves the lifting power of a person who radiates every cherished aspiration. Now comes the recognition that this is *inspiration*, that a real, living parent is here announcing, arms outstretched, "I am yours! And you are mine!"

A mother and father look down at their sleeping infant, in communing touch with what is sacred to both. Parental love, they see in this illumined moment, is not a shadow but a light of divine love in which splendor we became spirit children and by which we were enveloped.

The Spark of
Awakened Memories

Joseph F. Smith

Our knowledge of persons and things before we came here, combined with the divinity awakened within our souls through obedience to the gospel, powerfully affects . . . all our likes and dislikes, and guides our preferences in the course of this life, provided we give careful heed to the admonitions of the Spirit.

All those salient truths which come home so forcibly to the head and heart seem but the awakening of the memories of the spirit. Can we know anything here that we did not know before we came? Are not the means of knowledge in the first estate equal to those of this? I think that the spirit, before and after this probation, possesses greater facilities, aye, manifold greater, for the acquisition of knowledge, than while manacled and shut up in the prison house of mortality.

Had we not known before we came the necessity of our coming, the importance of obtaining tabernacles, the glory to be achieved in posterity, the grand object to be attained by being tried and tested—weighed in the balance, in the exercise of the divine attributes, god-like powers and free agency with which we are endowed; whereby, after descending below all things, Christ-like, we might ascend above all things, and become like our Father, Mother and Elder Brother, Almighty and Eternal!—we never would have come; that is, if we could have stayed away.

I believe that our Savior is the ever-living example to all flesh in all these things. He no doubt possessed a foreknowledge of all the vicissitudes through which he would have to pass in the mortal tabernacle, when the foundations of this earth were laid, "when the morning stars sang together, and all the sons of God shouted for joy" (Job 38:7). When he conversed with the brother of Jared, on the Mount, in his spiritual body, he understood his mission, and knew the work he had to do, as thoroughly as when he ascended from the Mount of Olives before the wondering gaze of the Jewish disciples, with his resurrected, glorious and immortal body.

. . . He is our example. . . . We are enjoined to follow him, as he followed his Head; that where he is, we may be also; and being with him, may be like him. If Christ knew beforehand, so did we. But in coming here, we forgot all, that our agency might be free indeed, to choose good or evil, that we might merit the reward of our own choice and conduct. But by the power of the Spirit, in the redemption of Christ, through obedience, we often catch a spark from the awakened memories of the immortal soul, which lights up our whole being as with the glory of our former home.

Free to Choose

Joseph Fielding Smith

God gave his children their free agency even in the spirit world, by which the individual spirits had the privilege, just as men have here, of choosing the good and rejecting the evil, or partaking of the evil to suffer the consequences of their sins. Because of this, some even there were more faithful than others in keeping the commandments of the Lord. Some were of greater intelligence than others, as we find it here, and were honored accordingly. . . .

. . . The spirits of men were not equal. They may have had an equal start, and we know they were all innocent in the beginning (D&C 93:38), but the right of free agency which was given to them enabled some to outstrip others and thus, through the eons of immortal existence, to become more intelligent, more faithful, for they were free to act for themselves, to think for themselves, to receive the truth or rebel against it. . . .

If there had been no free agency, there could have been no rebellion in heaven; but what would man amount to without this free agency? He would be no better than a mechanical contrivance. He could not have acted for himself, but in all things would have been acted upon, and hence unable to have received a reward for meritorious conduct. He would have been an automaton; could have had no "happiness nor misery, neither sense nor insensibility" (2 Nephi 2:11), and such could hardly be called existence.

Under such conditions there could have been no purpose in our creation.

The gospel plan is based upon the merit system, and such a system requires the free agency of man (D&C 29:35; 2 Nephi 2:16). Man may choose to do right or he may choose to do evil, for he is free "to choose liberty and eternal life, through the great Mediator of all men, or to choose captivity and death" (2 Nephi 2:27).

Essential to Our Progression

Bruce R. McConkie

In his infinite wisdom and goodness, the Eternal Father ordained laws by obedience to which his spirit children could advance and progress and eventually obtain the high reward of eternal life. These laws are the good news conveyed by God to his spirit progeny; they are the plan of salvation; they are the gospel of the Father. . . .

An all-wise Father endowed his spirit children with agency—the freedom and ability to choose good or evil—while they yet dwelt in his presence. Unless there are opposites—good and evil, virtue and vice, right and wrong—and unless intelligent beings are free to choose; free to obey or disobey; free to do good and work righteousness, or to walk in evil paths—unless this freedom exists, there can be no advancement and progression; no joy as contrasted with sorrow; no talents of one kind or another as contrasted with their absence; no eternal salvation as contrasted with eternal damnation. There can be no light unless there is darkness; no heat unless there is cold; no up unless there is down; no right unless there is left; no life unless there is death; and so on through all the realm of created and existent things. Opposites and agency are essential to existence and to progression. Without them there would be nothing.

Being subject to law, and having their agency, all the spirits of men, while yet in the Eternal Presence, developed aptitudes, talents, capacities, and abilities of every sort, kind, and degree. During the long expanse of life which then was, an infinite variety of talents and abilities came into being. As the ages rolled, no two spirits remained alike. Mozart became a musician; Einstein centered his interest in mathematics; Michelangelo turned his attention to painting. Cain, was a liar, a schemer, a rebel who maintained a close affinity to Lucifer. Abraham and Moses and all of the prophets sought and obtained the talent for spirituality. Mary and Eve were two of the greatest of all the spirit daughters of the Father. The whole house of Israel, known and segregated out from their fellows, was inclined toward spiritual things. And so it went through all the hosts of heaven, each individual developing such talents and abilities as his soul desired. . . .

There was as great a variety and degree of talent and ability among us there as there is among us here. Some excelled in one way, others in another. The Firstborn excelled all of us in all things.

On Earth and in Heaven

Brent L. Top

Premortal spirits had opportunities and requirements to be obedient, diligent, and faithful as do mortals on earth. They were expected to study and learn. . . . They were expected to be faithful in whatever commandments and duties the Father required of them. They were to develop talents, skills, and abilities that would enable them to live more productive and fulfilling lives, both there and here. They were to show love, kindness, patience, and consideration to their brothers and sisters. Each of these expectations is the same "as we find it here." Whatever other specific expectations and requirements existed there is not revealed. It certainly is logical to assume, however, that premortal spirits were expected to live the same gospel principles, with the exception of earthly ordinances, as men in the flesh. Scriptural passages such as Alma 13:3–4 seem to indicate that they exercised faith in Christ and the plan of redemption and repented there as men do here.

Since there must be opposition in order for agency to operate fully and since there was premortal goodness, there was also premortal wickedness. If there was premortal diligence and faithfulness, there must also have been premortal slothfulness, laziness, and disobedience just as there is in men here. . . .

. . . That gospel principles were taught and practiced . . . also implies that the atonement of Jesus Christ was in full effect in the premortal world. . . . This stimulating thought takes on additional significance when pondered in light of Alma's description of Christ's atonement as "an infinite and eternal sacrifice" (Alma 34:10).

"We Were There"

Sheri Dew

We cannot recall the "first lessons [we learned] in the world of spirits" (D&C 138:56) or the identities of our heavenly tutors and trainers who taught us perfectly. We can't remember what promises we made to ourselves, to others, and to the Lord. Nor can we remember our place in the Lord's heavenly kingdom or the spiritual maturity we achieved there. Thus, at times, we may feel more like "strangers and foreigners" than "fellowcitizens with the saints" (Ephesians 2:19).

There are, however, some remarkable things we *do* know. We know that *we were there*, in the heavenly councils before the foundations of this earth were laid. Said President Joseph F. Smith, "We were there; we were interested, and we took a part in this great preparation. We were unquestionably present in those councils . . . when Satan offered himself as a savior of the world if he could but receive the honor and glory of the Father for doing it. . . . We were, no doubt, there, and took part in all those scenes, we were vitally concerned in the carrying out of these great plans and purposes, we understood them, and it was for our sakes they were decreed, and are to be consummated" (*Gospel Doctrine*, 93–94).

We were there when our Father presented his plan, and we saw the Savior chosen and appointed—and, as the Prophet Joseph taught, we "sanctioned it" (*Teachings of the Prophet Joseph Smith*, 181). *We were there* among the heavenly host who sang and shouted for joy (Job 38:7). And when Satan unleashed his anger against the Father and the Son and was cast out of heaven, *we were there*, fighting on the side of truth. In fact, President George Q. Cannon said that we "stood loyally by God and by Jesus, and . . . *did not flinch*" (*Gospel Truth*, 7; emphasis added). We believed. We followed. And when we fought for truth in the most bitter of all confrontations, we did not flinch.

We were there. That means we existed. That means we were someone, that we as spirit children had identity and personality and the right to choose. Does it not therefore seem likely and logical that we had some kind of role in the premortal world before we came here? That we served each other and loved each other and led and taught and testified to each other? That we rallied and encouraged each other, and looked forward with enthusiasm to the high adventure of mortality? And that we were constantly learning and growing and preparing for the moment when our turn would arrive to embark upon our mortal sojourn?

Now we are here, separated from the safety of our heavenly home, serving a mission in this lone and dreary world—a mission designed to prove whether or not we want to be part of the kingdom of God more than we want anything else. The Lord is testing our faith and our integrity to see if we will persevere in a realm where Satan reigns. Happily, despite taking this test in a turbulent era of mortality, we have once again chosen to follow Christ. The Lord was speaking of us when he said, "My sheep hear my voice, . . . and they follow me" (John 10:27). We have *heard* his voice because we *remember* and *recognize* his voice.

Satan's So-Called Shortcut to Salvation

Robert J. Matthews

I think we often miss a major issue of the contention in premortality that eventually led to the war in heaven. We talk about it as though Satan were going to force everybody to obey when he said, "I will redeem all mankind, that one soul shall not be lost" (Moses 4:1)—we interpret that as meaning that he was proposing forced obedience.

It seems strange to me that a third of all the spirits that had the potential to be born into this world would have favored a proposal of forced obedience. Most of us do not like to be forced. As I see it, the issue was not so much one of force as it was that Satan said he would *guarantee* salvation for his spirit brothers and sisters. He promised salvation without excellence, without effort, without hard work, without individual responsibility, and without obedience to righteous laws. That is the lie he promulgated in the pre-earth councils. Satan does apply force sometimes, but his other ploy, salvation without repentance or obedience, was more attractive to many.

That so-called shortcut to salvation captivated many gullible and lazy spirits. They wanted something for nothing. We have certain aspects of that in our society today: something is offered for nothing (a free lunch, we sometimes call it), and certain kinds of subsidies promise to guarantee the reward without the effort. Obedience is not necessary when "anything goes" and there is no divine standard. With his something-for-nothing offer Satan led away many spirits.

But individual progress does not come that way. Only by serious and strenuous exertion do we improve in character and in spiritual growth. In our society we still come in contact with many who are influenced by this erroneous philosophy advocated by the rebellious in the premortal life. They think they can achieve salvation and exaltation without a struggle. We are still fighting the war in heaven with the same participants and the same issues, but we are fighting it on new territory.

Having ascertained that the devil's program was based on a false promise of excellence without effort (that is, without obedience), we can better appreciate the plan of our Father and his Chosen Son—a plan that would require real struggle on our part in order to do our best in this world to overcome our weaknesses and to obtain redemption from the effects of mortality. Such a redemption would be made possible through the sacrifice and merits of our Redeemer, Jesus Christ. It is in view of the premortal life and the issues fought in the war in heaven that everything else in the ministry of Jesus and in the gospel must be understood. If we overlook the premortal life, we never get the clear perspective necessary in mortality to understand the gospel of redemption.

The Ultimate Act of Love

Richard Eyre

The mortality plan was not without opposition. There were those who wanted less risk. They were led by a dark and demanding prince with his own agenda and a lust for power. He instilled fear by questioning the plan and our ability to participate successfully in it. If we left, how could we return? Freedom of choice encompassed the possibility of failure. . . . Would our bad decisions, our failures, our errors prevent us from making it back to God's presence and God's family? We understood that the price for the knowledge of mortal experience could be the loss of the very innocence that allowed us to live with God.

You and I may have been perplexed, but we were not persuaded by the opposition. We understood that without freedom and the risk it implied, the powerful purposes of mortality could not be fully realized or the godlike rewards fully obtained.

Despite the power of what our spirits had felt in learning of God's plan for mortality, the most magnificent moment and the deepest emotion were yet to come. Both came as the missing piece in the puzzle of the plan—as the overwhelming answer to our fearful question about how we could return. They came when one who was with God and who was God made a condescension beyond imagination, offering to sacrifice himself in a way that would bridge the chasm between God's realm and where we would find ourselves after our plunge into mortality. Using his own perfection as the ultimate collateral, he offered to pay our debts, to undergo the collective pain of all, and to somehow absorb and atone for all error and sin, making it possible for each of us to return. He offered to use his bounty to pay for our folly, his infinite perfection to compensate for our countless mistakes. He offered to do so at a price of pain beyond calculation or imagination.

The feelings unlocked in us by that condescension went beyond anything we had ever known. The generosity and power of the offered atonement filled us with awe. He who owed us nothing would give us everything. At the cost of unimaginable personal suffering, he would use his endless credits to balance our endless debits. He would give himself as a ransom in the ultimate act of love.

Falling to Mortality

Were it not for our transgression we never should

have had seed, and never should have known good and evil,

and the joy of our redemption, and the eternal life

which God giveth unto all the obedient.

MOSES 5:11

A Step Downward, yet Forward

Orson F. Whitney

In order that God's spirit children might have the opportunity to take bodies and undergo experiences on this earth, two heavenly beings came down in advance and became mortal for our sake. This is the true significance of the fall of Adam and Eve. It was not a mere yielding to temptation—they came on a mission, to pioneer this earthly wilderness, and open the way so that a world of waiting spirits might become souls, and make a stride forward in the great march of eternal progression. By the experience we gain here—the best of which comes from sorrow and tribulation—and by obedience to divine requirements, we accomplish successfully our earthly pilgrimage. We knew this in the life before, and rejoiced over it: "The morning stars sang together, and all the Sons of God shouted for joy" (Job 38:7) at the prospect—not of pain and death, but of eternal life and endless glory beyond!

The effect of the Fall was two-fold. It was a step downward, yet forward. The future prospect was glorious; but the present plight appalling. . . .

By Adam's fall the world was placed in pawn; the name of the pawnbroker was death, and his claim was twofold, involving the spirit as well as the body of man. No part of the thing pawned could be used as the means of redemption. Something not under the penalty of the broken law had to be given to mend that law, to balance the scale of justice, and restore the equilibrium of right. A holy being, one who had not sinned, who had not inherited the curse, gave his life as a ransom, to take the world out of pawn. That was the price of its freedom, and he whom we call Jesus Christ, paid the price, discharged the debt, when he descended from glory and was crucified in the Meridian of Time.

The Gift of Death, the Gift of Life

Bruce R. McConkie

Eternal life, the greatest of all the gifts of God, is available because of what Christ did in Gethsemane and at Golgotha. He is both the resurrection and the life. Immortality and eternal life are the children of the Atonement. . . .

But, be it remembered, the Atonement came because of the Fall. Christ paid the ransom for Adam's transgression. If there had been no Fall, there would be no Atonement with its consequent immortality and eternal life. Thus, just as surely as salvation comes because of the Atonement, so also salvation comes because of the Fall.

Mortality and procreation and death all had their beginnings with the Fall. The tests and trials of a mortal probation began when our first parents were cast out of their Edenic home. "Because that Adam fell, we are," Enoch said, "and by his fall came death; and we are made partakers of misery and woe" (Moses 6:48). . . .

And be it also remembered that the Fall was made possible because an infinite Creator, in the primeval day, made the earth and man and all forms of life in such a state that they could fall. This fall involved a change of status. All things were so created that they could fall or change, and thus was introduced the type and kind of existence needed to put into operation all of the terms and conditions of the Father's eternal plan of salvation.

This first temporal creation of all things . . . was paradisiacal in nature. In the primeval and Edenic day all forms of life lived in a higher and different state than now prevails. The coming fall would take them downward and forward and onward. Death and procreation had yet to enter the world. That death would be Adam's gift to man, and, then, the gift of God would be eternal life through Jesus Christ our Lord.

Thus, existence came from God; death came by Adam; and immortality and eternal life come through Christ.

Living by the Law of Obedience

Hugh Nibley

This world was organized in the light of infinite knowledge and experience and after due thought and discussion, to offer multiple facilities to an endless variety of creatures and especially to be the home and dominion of a godlike race who would take good care of it and have joy therein. Being a highly favored breed, much was expected of them, and their qualifications for advancement were to be put to the test by allowing an adversary, a common enemy to God and man, to tempt them and try them. It was decided before even the world was that, if man should yield to this temptation and thus lower his defenses and make himself vulnerable to repeated attacks of the adversary, steps would immediately be taken to put into operation a prearranged plan to restore him to his former status.

What God tells us in effect is, "Now that you have fallen and forfeited your paradise by deliberately, knowingly disobeying me, I will give you another chance, a chance to get back to that paradise by deliberately and knowingly obeying me. To get back where you were and beyond, you must repent—forever give up doing it your way, and decide to live by the law of God, or by the law of obedience, which means, doing it my way." Adam agreed to do it God's way, though Satan lost no time in trying to sell him on another plan. Adam's own children and their posterity, however, chose to [seek] salvation *their* way, not God's way, and ever since then there has been trouble.

The Problem and the Solution

Stephen E. Robinson

As the Fall separates us from God, so the Atonement reunites us with God. Therefore, without the Fall, the gospel would be unnecessary—like a hospital in a world where no one got sick or injured. The Fall is the problem to which the Atonement is the solution.

. . . Too many of us think of our problems as individual symptoms without understanding the underlying cause of our condition. We talk about "health problems," "I.Q. problems," "lack of willpower," or "trouble controlling my thoughts" without realizing that these are just isolated symptoms of a bigger problem—the fall of the human race. . . .

While the great victory of Jesus Christ over all our enemies has already been won, the natural effects of the Fall are nevertheless allowed to continue with us, and will continue until the Savior comes again to assert his ultimate lordship. Thus, while ultimate victory over our enemies is certain through Jesus Christ and in fact has already been won, we still have to wrestle with those enemies during our mortal lives. God intends that we struggle under these handicaps and limitations, for that is part of the test of mortality.

Reinstated to the Royal Family

Robert L. Millet

The plan of salvation, the great plan of happiness, is a system that provides for the salvation of individuals and the glorification of families. Families. That is what life here and hereafter is all about. We lived with God before we came here. God lives in the family unit, and we were and are part of that royal family. . . .

Spiritual death represents an alienation from God, a kind of disinheritance from the royal family. Unless reconciliation with the head of the family is made, the family name and its associated blessings may be lost. That is, unless an at-one-ment is brought to pass, we lose that family association and sociality, that family life of which the scriptures speak—eternal life. We then are without name and without family. We are spiritual orphans and thereby alone in the world. From an eternal perspective, in the words of Malachi, we have neither root (ancestry) nor branch (posterity) (Malachi 4:1). To experience the joys and feel the warmth and security known only in family living, we must be reinstated in the family, deemed worthy once again of the privileges and opportunities of being called a son or daughter of God.

Deliverance from this state—redemption from spiritual death—is made available only through the labors of a God, through the ministry of One mightier than death, One upon whom justice had no claims and death had no hold. Deliverance is not something that may be had without effort and without price. To be released from carnality and restored to righteousness, men and women must exercise saving faith in Jesus Christ and thus receive the blessings of the Atonement. They must put off the natural man through Christ, must crucify the old man of sin, and rise through their Redeemer unto a newness of life (Romans 6:6; Mosiah 3:19).

The Thorn and the Rose

Orson F. Whitney

Out of the tragedies of life issue our greatest blessings. There is compensation for every calamity. Not more surely does day follow night, than does joy succeed sorrow, and blessing follow blighting. . . .

What could have been more calamitous, from a human point of view, than the fall of our first parents, Adam and Eve? It brought death into the world. There was no death upon this planet till then, no pain, no sorrow. By the Fall, these misfortunes—if we may call them so—came upon the human family. But was it an unmixed evil? Did anything else result but sorrow, pain and trouble? . . .

. . . Our heavenly Father . . . has made plain to those who believe in the gospel of Jesus Christ that the fall of man was necessary: that by means of it the human race took a mighty stride forward—a downward step, yet a step upward, in the great march toward the goal of eternal life. Adam himself recognized this fact; Eve, his wife, recognized it, and it has crystalized into a doctrine which the Latter-day Saints accept as divine: "Adam fell that man might be, and man is that he might have joy" (see 2 Nephi 2:25).

Just as the thorn and the rose spring from the same stem, so joy and sorrow blend in mortal life; the bitter and the sweet are both essential to complete the round of human experience. Death has its mission, as well as life, and it is by contrast that we learn to appreciate. If there were no night, we could not appreciate the day; if there were no death, we would not know the value nor the significance of life eternal.

The fall of Adam and Eve was a terrible tragedy, but a wonderful blessing came from it; spirits became souls with opportunities for endless advancement.

Choose Wisely

Stephen E. Robinson

The Fall was neither a tragedy nor a mistake but a necessary step in the eternal progress of God's spirit children, for we had reached the point in our premortal growth where it was time to meet the opposition in a mortal setting, to encounter the evil and negative elements of existence, and to be sorted out according to our response to that opposition. Mortality is the sorting shed. Here some of us will pursue light most of the time no matter what the cost; some will pursue light some of the time if it doesn't cost too much; and others will prefer darkness. Unfortunately, our *real* preferences can be fairly tested only on a level playing floor, that is, in a place where light and darkness, good and evil, are both readily available to us equally, "for it must needs be, that there is an opposition in all things" (2 Nephi 2:11). Mortality is designed to offer those conditions.

Mortal life is like an all-you-can-eat buffet dinner with all the moral options spread out before us, from the pure, the virtuous, the righteous, and the holy at one end of the table to the abominable, the wicked, the corrupt, and the vile at the other end. Pick what you like; eat all you want; but your choices will unmistakably reveal what you prefer and therefore what you are. When we can have all we want of whatever we want, our choices unerringly reveal our true character. In this analogy, you are what you eat. In real life, you are what you *choose*.

Our Day to Do Our Best

Ezra Taft Benson

We once knew well our Elder Brother and his and our Father in Heaven. We rejoiced at the prospects of earth life that could make it possible for us to have a fulness of joy. We could hardly wait to demonstrate to our Father and our Brother, the Lord, how much we loved them and how we would be obedient to them in spite of the earthly opposition of the evil one.

Now we are here. Our memories are veiled. We are showing God and ourselves what we can do. Nothing is going to startle us more when we pass through the veil to the other side than to realize how well we know our Father and how familiar his face is to us.

God loves us. He is watching us. He wants us to succeed. We will know some day that he has not left one thing undone for the eternal welfare of each of us. If we only knew it, heavenly hosts are pulling for us—friends in heaven that we cannot now remember who yearn for our victory. This is our day to show what we can do—what life and sacrifice we can daily, hourly, instantly make for God. If we give our all, we will get his all from the greatest of all.

Give God your best, and his best will come back to you.

To Finish Is to Win

Anne Osborn Poelman

When we contemplate all the various aspects of our personalities that must become developed on the long pathway to perfection and exaltation, it is all too easy to despair when confronted with seemingly unreachable ideals. . . .

We are so often impatient with ourselves, forgetting that the Lord himself is infinitely patient. "Continue in patience until ye are perfected" (D&C 67:13), "run with patience the race" (Hebrews 12:1), and "add to temperance patience" (2 Peter 1:5–6) are words of eternal worth and wisdom, were we only to heed them. . . .

In our individual and collective quest for perfection, it is not the sprinter, the saint whose spirituality is only momentarily incandescent, who wins the eternal prize. Like running a marathon, to finish, to endure to the end, is to win. . . .

. . . Exaltation is not an instant process. Life is not leaping tall buildings at a single bound. It is more like carefully pacing ourselves, marshalling our precious energy and spiritual resources so that we *can* mount those steps one at a time. And perhaps we may even develop the eternal sense to pause a moment for rest, reflection, and contemplation of how far we've actually come. Then, as we resolutely turn our hearts and faces upwards, we rejoice in the wonders and delights that surely lie ahead.

Cultivating Heaven within Us

George Q. Cannon

[God's] reason for placing us here was to develop our divine natures. If we were not surrounded by darkness, we could not develop. We must taste the bitter in order to relish the sweet, that our spirits might be purified and that we might exercise our free agency. Good and evil must be presented before us. We are as free agents in our sphere as the angels are in theirs. We are free to do right or to do wrong and to choose the path we shall tread in. . . .

God will force no man to heaven, because we would be of no value if there. When we get to heaven it will be because we have developed within ourselves the qualities that make heaven. We must develop heaven within ourselves, so that there will be perfect harmony between us and our surroundings.

Selling the Summer Home in Babylon

Sharon G. Larsen

The Lord told Abraham that he sent us to earth to see if we would do what he asked us to do (Abraham 3:25). Choice becomes inescapable. . . . On the one hand, there is the reality of Satan, and on the other, the more powerful love of the Savior. . . .

Our faith and commitment are tested when the world offers tempting and enticing alternatives that can turn our faces from the Lord's kingdom. Some would like to live in that eternal city and still keep a "summer home" in Babylon. If we are not consciously and deliberately choosing the kingdom of God, we will in fact be moving backwards as the kingdom of God moves forward. . . .

Making right choices frees us and blesses us, even in choosing what may appear trivial in our lives. . . . Isn't it incredible? There are six billion people on this planet, and Heavenly Father cares what I watch for entertainment, and he cares what I eat and drink. He cares how I dress and how I earn and spend my money. He cares what I do and don't do. Heavenly Father cares about my happiness.

Our Father's caring comes in so many ways, and we have only to listen and live for it. Someone said, "If [we] have not chosen the Kingdom of God [first], it will in the end make no difference what [we] have chosen instead" (William Law, eighteenth-century clergyman).

The Bread of Adversity

Truman G. Madsen

How can good and bad fruit come from the same experience? The Divine and the devilish? It is the root of our spiritual nourishment that changes everything. That is the scale on which we came to be weighed.

Wrote B. H. Roberts, who identified with Joseph Smith as closely as did his blood brothers:

"Some of the lowliest walks in life, the paths which lead into the deepest valleys of sorrow and up to the most rugged steeps of adversity, are the ones which, if a man travel in, will best accomplish the object of his existence in this world. . . . The conditions which place men where they may always walk on the unbroken plain of prosperity and seek for nothing but their own pleasure, are not the best within the gift of God. For in such circumstances men soon drop into a position analogous to the stagnant pool; while those who have to contend with difficulties, brave dangers, endure disappointments, struggle with sorrows, eat the bread of adversity and drink the water of affliction, develop a moral and spiritual strength, together with a purity of life and character, unknown to the heirs of ease and wealth and pleasure. With the English bard, therefore, I believe: Sweet are the uses of adversity!" (*Gospel and Man's Relationship to Deity*, 289–90).

Yes, sweet, but bittersweet. "No chastening for the present seemeth to be joyous, but grievous: nevertheless afterward it yieldeth the peaceable fruit of righteousness unto them which are exercised thereby" (Hebrews 12:11).

... The message of the modern prophets, to a man (and none of them, if you look closely, has been spared any of the vicissitudes), is this: that there is meaning and purpose in all things we suffer; that "all these things" (D&C 122:7) can be for our good, however empty and barren they now appear. ... The Lord is not playing games with us. The outcome will far exceed the price; the "chastening" will be visioned as our blessing, the fiber of soul-quality will leave no regrets, only infinite and eternal gratitude, and the partnership we forged with him before we entered this refining fire will loom as marvelous to us as does the face of a loving mother in the eyes of a child who has just emerged from his fever . . . healed, alive, and prepared for life, eternal life, life like God's.

Sometimes He Will Not

Spencer W. Kimball

The Lord is omnipotent, with all power to control our lives, save us pain, prevent all accidents, drive all planes and cars, feed us, protect us, save us from labor, effort, sickness, even from death, if he will. But he will not. . . .

The basic gospel law is free agency and eternal development. To force us to be careful or righteous would be to nullify that fundamental law and make growth impossible. . . .

If we looked at mortality as the whole of existence, then pain, sorrow, failure, and short life would be calamity. But if we look upon life as an eternal thing stretching far into the pre-earth past and on into the eternal post-death future, then all happenings may be put in perspective

Is there not wisdom in his giving us trials that we might rise above them, responsibilities that we might achieve, work to harden our muscles, sorrows to try our souls? Are we not exposed to temptations to test our strength, sickness that we might learn patience, death that we might be immortalized and glorified?

If all the sick for whom we pray were healed, if all the righteous were protected and the wicked destroyed, the whole program of the Father would be annulled and the basic principle of the gospel, free agency, would be ended. No man would have to live by faith.

If joy and peace and rewards were instantaneously given the doer of good, there could be no evil—all would do good but not because of the rightness of doing good. There would be no test of strength, no development of character, no growth of powers, no free agency, only satanic controls.

Should all prayers be immediately answered according to our selfish desires and our limited understanding, then there would be little or no suffering, sorrow, disappointment, or even death, and if these were not, there would also be no joy, success, resurrection, eternal life, or godhood. "For it must needs be, that there is an opposition in all things . . . righteousness . . . wickedness . . . holiness . . . misery . . . good . . . bad . . ." (2 Nephi 2:11).

Being human, we would expel from our lives physical pain and mental anguish and assure ourselves of continual ease and comfort, but if we were to close the doors upon sorrow and distress, we might be excluding our greatest friends and benefactors. Suffering can make saints of people as they learn patience, long-suffering, and self-mastery. The sufferings of our Savior were part of his education. "Though he were a Son, yet learned he obedience by the things which he suffered; and being made perfect, he became the author of eternal salvation unto all them that obey him" (Hebrews 5:8–9).

The Plan and the Work

Hugh Nibley

The gospel and the Church: we call one the *plan* and the other the *work*. The plan looks to the eternities and must necessarily be perfect; but the *work is right here and is anything but the finished product*. Yet the two are inseparable! "To bring to pass the immortality and eternal life of man" is the *plan*; to carry it out, "*this* is my *work* and my glory" (Moses 1:39)—the glory is in the work.

We are permitted to take part in the work, to participate like eager but bungling children in the kitchen or the shop—dropping things, doing it all wrong, quarreling, getting in each other's way, trying the patience of indulgent elders. What a headache! Yet such is the best and happiest arrangement for all concerned, everybody having a wonderful time—and it is found only in the restored Church, where the plan and the work are equally exhilarating and equally sacred.

Saviors on Mount Zion

John A. Widtsoe

In our preexistent state, in the day of the great council, we made a certain agreement with the Almighty. The Lord proposed a plan, conceived by him. We accepted it. Since the plan is intended for all men, we become parties to the salvation of every person under that plan. We agreed, right then and there, to be not only saviors for ourselves, but measurably saviors for the whole human family. We went into a partnership with the Lord. The working out of the plan became then not merely the Father's work, and the Savior's work, but also our work. The least of us, the humblest, is in partnership with the Almighty in achieving the purpose of the eternal plan of salvation.

That places us in a very responsible attitude towards the human race. By the doctrine, with the Lord at the head, we become saviors on Mount Zion, all committed to the great plan of offering salvation to the untold numbers of spirits. To do this is the Lord's self-imposed duty, this great labor his highest glory. Likewise, it is man's duty, self-imposed, his pleasure and joy, his labor, and ultimately his glory.

There is no place for forgetting the other man in the gospel of the Lord Jesus Christ. There stands my brother; it was for him that the whole plan was made, for him the Church was organized, for him all these blessings were given—not for me alone. Oh, I stand there, too. The Church was made for me, the gospel was given for me, all the blessings were given for me; but my brother is entitled to them just as much as I am. He and I together and all of us must unitedly work together to fulfill the great purposes of the Almighty Father.

Following the
Lord's Perfect Formula

Mark E. Petersen

Recently I passed a beautiful stone church. In front of it was a neat little bulletin board announcing the pastor's sermon topic for the next Sunday and asking the question "Where are you going to spend eternity?" . . .

. . . I ask you: Where are you really going? Where is your family going? . . . Are you always going to be together like you are now? Do you ever think of eternity? . . .

I think that we must all accept the fact that whereas God is a most merciful Father—infinitely so—he also is a just God. And do you recall what he wants of us?

He hopes that we will all become like him, just as the Savior commanded in his Sermon on the Mount (Matthew 5:48). As the children of God, we have within us the full capability of becoming like him. Isn't it natural for children to become like their parents? But we can't become like him merely through wishful thinking, nor even by being what we ourselves may call good.

He has his own plan for us to follow, and it alone will assure us the desired results. It is a formula for success both in this life and the life to come. Unless we follow it, we restrict ourselves. It is that way in everything else, isn't it? Do you remember when you studied chemistry in school? What happened if you didn't follow the formula in a laboratory experiment? Do you remember also in school that you were required to follow the curriculum or you couldn't graduate? It is the same with eternity. We have to follow the Lord's formula, which is his gospel. . . .

But the Lord knows that perfection cannot come by imperfect means, and therefore he gives us his perfect formula, with the warning—such as we also were given in school—that unless we follow it, unless we fully accept his plan, we cannot receive the blessing.

. . . Obedience is a part of greatness. It is only good sense to comply with divine law. . . .

Don't you see that if we are going to spend eternity with the Lord, we have to earn that privilege by doing what he asks of us? If we are going to spend eternity with him, we must become like him and so must our wives and our children. But we only become like him by keeping his commandments, by being in his church and following his program. . . .

We are told that we shall reap as we sow. This is the law of the harvest. If we sow wheat on our farms here on earth, we grow wheat. If, in our character building, we sow the seeds of righteousness, we shall reap that kind of harvest. So as the Lord himself said: "Whatsoever ye sow, that shall ye also reap; therefore, if ye sow good ye shall also reap good for your reward" (D&C 6:33).

The Greatest Hope

Anita R. Canfield

During family home evening I told my family I wanted to go to the celestial kingdom. It was the most important thing to me. Then Steve said, "Me too. In fact, that's the whole reason your mother and I got married. We wanted to go to the celestial kingdom, and we knew we could help each other get there." Ashley voiced the same desire, as did Chase. All this time, Paige, who was then five years old, looked concerned. Finally she blurted out, "Wait a minute, everybody. I want to go too, but I don't know where it is!"

Steve picked her up and said, "Paige, none of us knows where it is really. That's why we have to follow Jesus. He knows *the way!*"

"I am *the way*" (John 14:6; emphasis added). He is *the way* to hope and faith and peace. He is the way home, even home to eternal life.

Eternal life does not mean immortality. Everyone will be resurrected and have immortality. Eternal is one of God's names. Eternal life is to have the kind of life God has. It is to inherit all that the Father has. But it is much, much more even than that. It is to become like Jesus Christ—to possess every attribute, every sympathy, every quality, every bit of divinity possessed by the Savior himself. It is to be all that we struggle and stretch to be in this life—and more. It is to be free from the pains and chains of weakness and to be full of the love of God. It is the greatest hope there is.

Priorities, Perspectives, and Promises

Cheer up your hearts, and remember that

ye are free to act for yourselves —

to choose the way of everlasting

death or the way of eternal life.

2 NEPHI 10:23

Unlocking Our Memories

Truman G. Madsen

We once dwelt in the scintillating presence of the Eternal Father. So rich, so exquisite was our condition there (though it was not without conflict) that we can hardly endure remembering. . . . Our mortal amnesia is the Lord's anesthesia. We must stay in this condition to work out our possibilities, undergo the stress and distress that lead to perfection.

One role of Christ, as of his prophets, is to remind us— to "bring all things to our remembrance" (see John 14). Brigham Young taught that we are totally familiar with God the Father, but that knowledge is "locked up" within us. Nothing, he said, will so much astound us "when our eyes are open in eternity, as to think that we were so stupid in the body" (Harold B. Lee, *Youth and the Church*, 50). Lorenzo Snow taught that "according to our preparation there"—and he taught that our preparation was exactly suited to our anticipated missions—"our flesh was to become acquainted with our experiences in the spirit." . . . Only when we are touched by the Spirit do we overcome, for a fleeting time, our memory imprisonment. Then, as Joseph F. Smith puts it, "we are lighted up with the glory of our former home" (see *Gospel Doctrine*, 13). . . .

We have flashes—the French phrase is *déjà vu*, which literally translated means "already seen." We cry out, " I have anticipated this." And there are other wonderings— haunting landscapes, the sounds of music that are echoes of eternity, a love for the truth ("my sheep know my voice"), and spiritual acquaintanceship. . . . We have great gifts, greater endowments, and the greatest of destinies. The gold is in the mine. But the power of Christ must sink a shaft to bring it out. In the end our becoming depends on pre-tastes or, quite literally, after-tastes.

A morning is ahead when there will be brightness and glory exceeding all prior mornings, and a "perfect bright recollection." Then, we are promised, we will be given back our lost memory and with it our selves. The key will fit the door. As the earth will become an instrument of truth whereby "all things for [our] glory, past, present and future" (D&C 130:7) will be manifest, so we will become living Urim and Thummim. We will not just begin to see. We will see it all. "The day shall come when you shall comprehend even God, being quickened in him by him" (D&C 88:49). To comprehend God is to comprehend all that God comprehends, to "see as [we] are seen, and know as [we] are known" (D&C 76:94). If in this world our spirits still sing in the afterburn of that exposure, how, with "spirit and element, inseparably connected," (D&C 93:33) we shall sing a new, more glorious song in his eternal presence! Surely a climactic scene awaits all of us.

The Promise of Forever

Spencer W. Kimball

We are eternal beings. We have no way of comprehending how long we dwelt in the presence of God as his spirit children. We are here in mortality for a moment of testing and trial. Then we will come forth in the resurrection, receive an inheritance in whatever kingdom we deserve, and go on living the commandments to all eternity.

This life consists of a brief yesterday, a few short hours of today, and a few moments tomorrow. The oldest men among us scarcely live longer than a hundred years. But the life that is to be is forever. It will have no end. Men will rise from the grave and not die after. Life is eternal, unending; never after the resurrection will the children of our Father taste death.

We have a hope in Christ here and now. He died for our sins. Because of him and his gospel, our sins are washed away in the waters of baptism; sin and iniquity are burned out of our souls as though by fire; and we become clean, have clear consciences, and gain that peace which passeth understanding (Philippians 4:7).

. . . The gospel blesses us today. But today is just a grain of sand in the Sahara of eternity. We have also a hope in Christ for the eternity that lies ahead; otherwise, as Paul said, we would be "of all men most miserable" (1 Corinthians 15:19).

How great would be our sorrow—and justly so—if there were no resurrection! How miserable we would be if there were no hope of life eternal! If our hope of salvation and eternal reward should fade away, we would certainly be more miserable than those who never had such an expectancy. . . .

We have an eternal hope in Christ. We know this life is given us to prepare for eternity, "and that same sociality which exists among us here will exist among us there, only it will be coupled with eternal glory, which glory we do not now enjoy" (D&C 130:2).

Crossing the Chasm

Cheryl Brown Mitchell

The covenants we make on this earth are designed to
lead us through our complexities and help us decide what to
do when we do not understand, or when demands press upon
us, or when we feel as if we cannot hold on one second
longer. We are invited to lift up our hearts and rejoice and
to cleave unto the covenants we have made. They are sure
sources of guidance and strength. . . .

Christ, through whom we make our covenants, understands fully their purposes. He also fully understands the
complexities of our lives not only because he helped fashion
the plan for this earth, but also because he experienced the
tests and complexities of mortality himself. . . . Christ himself speaks of his experiences: "Which suffering caused
myself, even God, the greatest of all, to tremble because of
pain, and to bleed at every pore, and to suffer both body and
spirit—and would that I might not drink the bitter cup, and
shrink" (D&C 19:18). . . . Does he understand us when we
suffer and shrink at our tests? Does he know what it feels like
when we cannot bear one second more? Does he know what
it means to have to go forward without fully understanding
how all the pieces fit in our missions, our lives? Does he
know what it means to cleave unto a covenant when things
are the darkest, the hardest? . . .

Because our Savior experienced mortality, we can trust
that he understands . . . personally how difficult tests can be.
But, more important, through the keeping of his premortal

covenant, he has made it possible for us to keep ours. His example shows us the way; his atonement redeems us from our weaknesses, faults, and failings. . . .

I once climbed with a group of friends to the top of Lady Mountain in Zion Canyon. The trail was treacherous. There were steep drop-offs in places. There were places where trail-builders had cut steps into the side of the mountain or placed chains for climbers to hold on to. After working our way up the difficult trail, we finally reached the "almost top." We could see the top, but reaching it required a leap across a very deep chasm, a chasm which, although narrow, plunged dangerously to the valley floor.

For many years the climb up Lady Mountain has been for me an analogy of how our Savior and our covenant relationship to him work. My part of the covenant relationship is the climb up the mountain. Although it can be dangerous and difficult, I must persevere. Although there are some slips and occasional backtracking to return to the trail, I climb. And even though I keep climbing, I will only reach the "almost top," where, because of my sins, there will be a chasm between where I am and where I want to go.

That is where Christ's part of the covenant relationship comes in, because "it is by grace that we are saved, after all we can do" (2 Nephi 25:23). He has been on the trail before us and with us, building the path, placing commandments and covenants, easing the climb all the way up. And when we reach the top and see the depth of the chasm created by our sins and the justice of God, Christ is there, the sure hand across an unfathomable separation. He reaches out because, in his covenant with us, he has promised to lift us across.

The Second Act

Ardeth G. Kapp

Each of us is on stage for a time. This is not the first nor the final act. It is the second act, and we have been assured that we performed our first act very well. . . .

As we participate in this great drama of earth life, we often find that the parts we so much desire may not be available to us for a time. We find ourselves placed in other roles, only to discover after some years and after a trial of our faith that those other roles may even be the very ones we auditioned for, roles for which we received coaching and divine guidance from our Heavenly Father before we left our heavenly home to come on stage for a season.

President George Q. Cannon gives us great insight as he explains, "God has chosen us out of the world and has given us a great mission. I do not entertain a doubt myself that we were selected and fore-ordained for the mission before the world was, that we had our parts allotted to us in this mortal state of existence as our Savior had his assigned to him" (*Gospel Truth*, 18). . . .

As participants on the stage of life, we . . . must be sensitive to timing, and we must work to support each other. There are times when some will, for a brief moment, move center stage in front of the lights, then go backstage or even offstage into the wings for a time, confident that the entire cast will participate in the final curtain call. . . .

Even as we endeavor to play our various parts in their appropriate seasons, there will continually be self-appointed stage managers who, not knowing or caring about the script, will shout from the wings, "You're playing the wrong part. You don't want the supporting role. That isn't important. Why be a supporting actor when you can be the star? Be front stage. Move in. Let them know who you are. This is your chance to win the applause." . . .

There are always loud voices assuming authorship while abdicating stewardship. You and I may never win acclaim, and society may never know us beyond the street where we live, or because one calling or position may be in the public eye more than another. But I am sure that when the lights have gone out and the curtain is closed on our second act, the opinions of others, the acceptance and applause of the crowd, will be a haunting echo if our Father's approval is in question.

It won't matter if we play center stage or in the wings if our Lord and Savior is at the very center of our life.

The Test, the Task, the Commandment

Ezra Taft Benson

The *great test of life* is obedience to God. "We will prove them herewith," said the Lord, "to see if they will do all things whatsoever the Lord their God shall command them" (Abraham 3:25).

The *great task of life* is to learn the will of the Lord and then do it.

The *great commandment of life* is to love the Lord.

"Come unto Christ," exhorts Moroni in his closing testimony, " . . . and love God with all your might, mind and strength" (Moroni 10:32).

This, then, is the first and great commandment. "Thou shalt love the Lord thy God with all thy heart, and with all thy soul, and with all thy mind, and with all thy strength" (Mark 12:30; see also Deuteronomy 6:5; Matthew 22:37; Luke 10:27; Moroni 10:32; D&C 59:5).

It is the pure love of Christ, called charity, that the Book of Mormon testifies is the greatest of all—that never faileth, that endureth forever, that all men should have, and that without which they are nothing (Moroni 7:44–47; 2 Nephi 26:30).

"Wherefore, my beloved brethren," pleads Moroni, "pray unto the Father with all the energy of [your] heart, that ye may be filled with this love, which he hath bestowed upon all who are true followers of his Son, Jesus Christ; that ye may become the sons of God; that when he shall appear we shall be like him" (Moroni 7:48). . . .

To love God with all your heart, soul, mind, and strength is all-consuming and all-encompassing. It is no lukewarm endeavor. It is total commitment of our very being—physically, mentally, emotionally, and spiritually—to a love of the Lord.

The breadth, depth, and height of this love of God extend into every facet of one's life. Our desires, be they spiritual or temporal, should be rooted in a love of the Lord. Our thoughts and affections should be centered on the Lord. "Let all thy thoughts be directed unto the Lord . . . forever" (Alma 37:36).

Why did God put the first commandment first? Because he knew that if we truly loved him we would want to keep all of his other commandments. "For this is the love of God," says John, "that we keep his commandments" (1 John 5:3; see 2 John 1:6).

We must put God in the forefront of everything else in our lives. He must come first, just as he declares in the first of his Ten Commandments: "Thou shalt have no other gods before me" (Exodus 20:3).

When we put God first, all other things fall into their proper place or drop out of our lives. Our love of the Lord will govern the claims of our affection, the demands on our time, the interests we pursue, and the order of our priorities.

"Preparation for Joys Eternal"

Parley P. Pratt

O candidates for celestial glory! Would your joys be full in the countless years of eternity without forming the connections, the relationship, the kindred ties which concentrate in the domestic circle, and branch forth, and bud and blossom, and bear the fruits of eternal increase?

Would [you] . . . be satisfied to enjoy in "single blessedness," without an increase of posterity, those exhaustless stores of never ending riches and enjoyments? Or, would you, like your Heavenly Father, prompted by eternal benevolence and charity, wish to fill countless millions of worlds, with your begotten sons and daughters, and to bring them through all the gradations of progressive being, to inherit immortal bodies and eternal mansions in your several dominions?

If such be your aspirations, remember that this present probation is the world of preparation for joys eternal. This is the place where family organization is first formed for eternity. . . .

Here, in the holy temples and sanctuaries of our God, must the everlasting covenants be . . . sealed, bound and recorded in the holy records, [for both the living and the dead,] and guarded and preserved in the archives of God's Kingdom. . . .

Here, in the holy sanctuary, must be revealed, ordained and anointed the kings and queens of eternity. . . .

This is heaven's eternal law, as revealed to the ancients of all ages, who held the keys of eternal priesthood, after the order of the Son of God; and, as restored with the priesthood of the saints of this age.

"Let the World Go"

Sheri Dew

Prophets have admonished us to forsake the world and turn our hearts to Jesus Christ, who promised us, "In this world your joy is *not* full, but in *me* your joy is full" (D&C 101:36; emphasis added). Said President Spencer W. Kimball, "If we insist on spending all our time and resources building up . . . a worldly kingdom, that is exactly what we will inherit" (*Ensign*, June 1976, 6). How often are we so focused on pursuing the so-called good life that we lose sight of eternal life? It is the fatal spiritual equivalent of selling our birthright for a mess of pottage.

The Lord revealed the remedy for such spiritual disaster when he counseled Emma Smith to "lay aside the things of this world, and seek for the things of a better" (D&C 25:10). And Christ provided the pattern, declaring prior to Gethsemane, "I have *overcome* the world" (John 16:33; emphasis added). The only way that *we* may overcome the world is by coming unto Christ. And coming unto Christ means walking away from the world. It means placing Christ and Christ only at the center of our lives so that the vanities and philosophies of men lose their addictive appeal. Satan *is* the god of Babylon, or this world. Christ is the God of Israel, and his atonement gives us power to overcome the world. "If you expect glory, intelligence and endless lives," said President Joseph F. Smith, "*let the world go*" (*Teachings of Presidents of the Church: Joseph F. Smith* [1998], 243; emphasis added).

As sisters in Zion we can be obstacles to the adversary's conspiracy against families and virtue. No wonder he tempts us to settle for earthly pleasures rather than to seek for eternal glory. A forty-five-year-old mother of six told me recently that when she stopped poring over magazines that plagued her with images of how her home and wardrobe should look, she began to feel more at peace. She said, "I may be chubby, gray, and wrinkled, but I am a chubby, gray, wrinkled daughter of God, who knows me and loves me."

To Behold the Face of God

Hugh Nibley

What are we afraid of? What do men fear most? Believe it or not, it is joy. Against joy, society erects its most massive bulwarks. The gospel is a message of terrifying joy. What is the culmination of all joy? To stand in the presence of God and behold his face—we don't need to argue that point. Yet what is the most frightening prospect that mortal man can imagine? Certainly, to stand in the presence of God and behold his face!

The presence of Jesus was an unbearable torment to wicked men and devils alike; rather than look upon the face of the Lord, the wicked shall beg the rocks and the mountains to cover them; the apostles who cheerfully faced death at the hands of devilish men were "sore afraid" (Matthew 17:6) at the approach of God the Father on the mountain; and when Moses descended from another mountain, the people fell down in deadly fear at the presence of one who had been talking face to face with God, though Moses himself at an earlier time had "hid his face; for he was afraid to look upon God" (Exodus 3:6). It is not hell that men fear most, but heaven.

Plainly the joy for which man was created is no light and trivial thing. It has more substance to it than all the rest of our existence. We live here, as many a philosopher has noted, in a shadow world of half-lights and unrealities. Everything in our society conspires to dampen and control joy. Our sordid little pleasures are carefully channeled and commercialized; our pitiful escapes to alcohol and drugs are a plain admission that we will not allow ourselves to have joy in our right senses. Only little children can face up to it—they have no hidden guilt to admonish cautious behavior or make joy appear unseemly. The kingdom of heaven is one of joy, and it is literally true that unless we are as little children we cannot possibly inherit it. . . .

If the world is a dark and dreary place, it is because we prefer it that way, for there is nothing in the world that can keep a man from joy if joy is what he wants. Direct access to our Father in Heaven through prayer is always open. But right there we draw back; as soon as we gain a distant glimpse of it, we are not so sure whether we want this joy. It is altogether too much for us to bear.

We must learn by degrees to live with it. It is not strange that we are afraid of so great and overpowering a thing—that we are overawed by the feeling that all this is too good for us. The fact is that it *is* too good for us—much too good, and the message of the prophets and the Church to us here is that we must awake and prepare ourselves as good and faithful servants to enter into the *joy* of the Lord. We are not ready yet. . . .

That we may come to support not the burden of great suffering, but the much greater impact of limitless joy is the purpose of our training here. "In the world ye shall have tribulation," says the Lord to his prophets, "but be of good cheer; I have overcome the world" (John 16:33).

The Road to Joy

Hugh B. Brown

Too many go through life with eyes closed, with ears stopped, with sense of feeling deadened or never awakened, and with the shutters closed to the windows of the soul, so absorbed in material things that they miss the beauty and the richness which lie about them. God's glory is intelligence, and we must climb the ladder of knowledge if we are ever to share that glory.

"Fools believe," says the philosopher, "that if they can only achieve wealth, their wishes will be completely gratified. A man of means is supposed to be a man with means for the fulfilment of every desire. A life devoted to the acquisition of wealth is useless unless one knows how to turn it into joy, and that is an art that requires culture and wisdom. A succession of sensual pursuits never satisfies for long. One must understand the ends of life as well as the art of acquiring means. Men are a thousand times more intent upon becoming rich than on acquiring culture, though it is quite certain that what a man *is* contributes more to his happiness than what he has; not wealth but wisdom is the way."

He who finds joy in life does not speak of its relationships as duties, obligations, and responsibilities. To him life is a privilege and an opportunity to serve. Service leads to love, and love, the fulfilment of the great commandment, leads to immortality and eternal progress. Here alone may joy be found.

The road to this desirable goal may lead through valleys

of sorrow and pain and disappointment, but the prize is worth the price. Great souls in all ages have been willing to accept poverty, obscurity, and persecution rather than forsake the quest. They knew the joy of self-sacrificing service.

Yes, man is that he might have joy—the joy of conquest over self; the joy of achievement; the joy of having fought the good fight; of having kept the faith; the joy of a peace that is earned; the joy of increase; the joy of living that more abundant life exemplified by the Master; the joy that comes from patient continuance in well-doing; the joy of comradeship; the joy of awareness and appreciation.

That joy which is the purpose of our being could not have been achieved without the refining fires of life's experience. If man had remained in that untried, innocent state of pre-existent infancy, he would have done no good, for he knew no evil, would have had no joy, for he knew no sorrow.

Man is, then, that he might have that joy which comes through understanding and obeying those eternal laws upon which all blessings are predicated.

God's First Question

Richard Eyre

While mortality with all its choices is a test, the goal or purpose of the test is joy. . . . God's commandments are *loving counsel from a wise Father*. He knows the ingredients and the makeup of true and lasting joy, and he gives us that formula through his laws and commandments, along with a world that is filled with opportunities for the joy he sent us here to find.

I have a wonderful old friend, a rural country doctor, who shares my convictions about a life before life. I love to go on road trips with him and talk about life and ideas and philosophy. On one such drive he asked me, "What do you think will be God's first question to you on judgment day?" I surmised that it would have something to do with how well I'd done keeping God's commandments. "I doubt it," he said. "I think the first question will be about the goal, not about the plan. The commandments are his plan, his way. The goal—his goal for us—is *joy*. I think he'll want to know how much joy we found down here. He'll say, 'How much did you enjoy those mountains I made for you, or those seacoasts, or those sunsets? How much joy did you have in your marriage and your family? How much joy did you give others?'"

If God made the world for our joy, then the most important measurement of our accomplishments here is how much real joy we found. Did we figure out that his commandments were a plan for maximizing our joy? Did we live that plan? Did we find the joy?

Consecrate the Everyday

Joan B. MacDonald

Words cannot describe the joy we feel when we learn to see the vast and the beautiful in our daily lives. Each time we perceive the miraculous, each time we appreciate beauty, each time we feel love, each time our problems result in our personal growth, each time we experience strength or crea‑ tivity in our work, each breath we take, each step we walk presents us with manifestations of the grace, the goodness, and the greatness of our Heavenly Father. Worship him.

Worship him with words of gratitude and praise but wor‑ ship him with your actions also . . . , not just the service actions that we normally think we can offer to God, but all of our actions. . . . To consecrate means to give all that we have and do to God. Consecration of our life to God is the only response possible for those who truly perceive God's goodness. . . .

To consecrate our lives to God means we value nothing more than we value him and his service. . . .

To consecrate our lives to God means we have no priority higher than knowing and serving and becoming one with God. . . .

To consecrate our lives to God means to bring every thought to the obedience of Christ. Consecration invites Christ to walk with us through our daily days. Consecration invites Christ into our jobs, our housework, our parenting, our marriages, our friendships, and our church and com‑ munity service. Consecration sees Christ and godliness expressed in our jobs, our housework, our parenting, our marriages, our friendships, and our service. Consecration surrenders all to God and sees God in everything and everywhere. Consecration makes each moment of our lives moments of worship. Consecration sanctifies our life and makes it holy. . . .

. . . The issues of life are God's issues. Everyday life, everyday tasks, everyday worries and concerns, everyday triumphs and despairs, everyday lessons and learning, everyday moments, no matter how mundane, all belong to God.

It is with food, the pen, the hammer, the mop, and the checkbook; in the kitchen and in the office, in the yard and in the living room; with the child, with the boss, with the neighbor that we truly worship God, and our hearts, minds, souls, and lives are sanctified.

If we allow it, our everyday days are holy days, our everyday nights are holy nights, and our everyday life is truly holiness to the Lord.

Eternal Life Is Now

Mary B. Kirk

Your circumstances and work may be very different from mine, but you can find holiness in them (Mosiah 18:12). . . .

It took a great insight from my husband and a personal revelation to me to finally fix in my mind the fact that eternal life doesn't start at the Savior's second coming, that it's right now. Our relationship with God and Christ goes back all the way and it goes forward all the way and today is part of it. We need to think about each day as being an integral part of the great picture. In other words, the mere fact that we are *alive today* is holy in itself. We chose to participate in mortality. So let's "rejoice and be glad" (Psalm 118:24) in it, and acknowledge our stewardship over each day, and *feel* each day's potential for holiness.

In one Bill Keane "Family Circus" comic strip, Dolly and Jeffy are sitting high on a hill looking out over things. Dolly has her arm around Jeffy's shoulders, and he's looking teachable and very intent upon what she is saying. The wisdom of her words has helped me find holiness many times since I first read it. She explains, "Yesterday is the *past*, tomorrow is the *future*, and today is a *gift*. That's why they call it the *present*." God is the author of the past and the future, and he's the giver of the present gift. He'll sprinkle holiness into today, and we will find it. He will pour out his holiness upon us at the rate that we open our eyes and perceive, open our ears and understand, and open our hearts and invite him in. And then we'll become like him.

All the Way Home

Elaine L. Jack

How do we press forward on the straight and narrow way? How do we focus on our eternal progression when we live in a world that demands such attention to daily tasks? . . .

Remember, our eternal progression is the very essence of our earthly existence. It is the Lord's plan to get us all the way home to our Father in Heaven. This I know: Each of us can get there from here. . . .

Elder Neal A. Maxwell has said, "There are no separate paths back to that heavenly home. Just one straight and narrow way, at the end of which, though we arrive trailing tears, we shall at once be 'drenched in joy'" (*Ensign*, May 1978, 11).

Indeed, the path is not soft, green grass; it is not without hardship and heartache. It is often an uphill climb strewn with rocks, many of them in the shape of mighty boulders. We can't predict what our challenges will be because our lives are all different. Though the path is narrow, our moves are not scripted. There are diversions which attempt to lure us from the straight and narrow. It is our covenants that are the road signs to eternal life. Just as it is more difficult to read the signs on the main road from a side street, so too it is more difficult to hear the still, small voice of warnings, rough road ahead, when we have distanced ourselves from our covenants.

When the Lord says "walk with me" (Moses 6:34), he is asking us to become more spiritual by being obedient to his word. Developing spirituality is critical to our eternal progress. . . .

Focusing on our eternal purposes can ease our burdens and make our lives happy and more productive. . . .

We know why we are here. When we are on the path, we can feel it. The fruits of eternal progress are manifest in joy, peace, love, hope, increased confidence in the Lord. Though the path is narrow, it is sure. It is on this path that we testify daily of our love for the Lord, his children, his church, his counsel, and the richness of his blessings. By our good works we magnify what is mighty in us all, one step at a time, one day at a time, all the time.

We know the path; in fact, we know it well. The prophet Nephi promised, "If ye shall press forward, feasting upon the word of Christ, and endure to the end, behold, thus saith the Father: Ye shall have eternal life" (2 Nephi 31:20). May it be so.

A Light in the Storm

Margaret D. Nadauld

It was just a few days before Christmas, and we were newlyweds traveling home for the holidays. . . . We had been on the road all day and most of the night when we came upon a terrible snowstorm. We found ourselves in a blinding blizzard, and the snow was growing deeper on the highway with each passing moment. The night was pure black. We couldn't see where we were going, and because of the deep snow we couldn't see the lines on the road. . . .

Suddenly in front of us we began to see a huge semitruck going slowly and steadily ahead. We could barely make out his taillights, but seeing them gave us hope. My husband, who was driving, fixed his eyes on the lights from the truck, and we drove along in the tracks it made through the deepening snow. Our panic subsided somewhat with that guide up ahead, because he knew the route, he sat up higher than we and could have a better view, and surely he had communication equipment if it was needed.

With prayers on our lips and white-knuckled hands holding on, we followed that light through the storm. We passed many cars off both sides of the road before we sensed that the truck was slowing down and pulling off the highway. In an act of faith, we followed him and soon found ourselves, to our great relief, in a place of safety, a place of refuge. . . . We could hardly wait to tell the driver of the truck how grateful we were for his help—for leading the way.

We are each one on a road going toward home, but we're not trying to get there for Christmas. We're trying to get there for eternity. We want to arrive home safely to our loving Father in Heaven. He wants us to make it safely there, so he has sent a guiding light for us to follow: a Savior, the Lord Jesus Christ, the perfect example. He knows the way. He lights our path in the dark of night, in storms, at crossroads, and in the daylight. He is always ready to show the way back home.

Remember What We Forgot

Ardeth G. Kapp

Lest we forget, the grand plan is designed entirely to help us return to our Father in Heaven. . . .

One of the most comforting and reassuring thoughts for me through the years has been, "I chose to come here; I sided with Christ's plan rather than Satan's in the premortal existence." We knew before we were born that we would experience joys and sorrows on this earth, and we eagerly accepted the plan. . . .

It is absolutely essential to our progress that we remember this truth: We made this choice before we arrived here. Wonderfully reassuring scriptures give evidence of many who accepted the blotting out of premortal memory, exercised their faith, kept the commandments, and were assured of their salvation. The road to that eternal salvation requires that we be tried and tested along the way (D&C 136:31). . . .

Yes, there is a forgetting, but thankfully there's also a remembering, and it is crucial to our inner peace and well-being. . . .

This life is the time to work and to save and to prepare and, yes, to deny ourselves some things so that we can travel home. The gospel principles help give us a vision of that home. They tell us what to do, how to save, where to buy the ticket, and how much it will cost. A current temple recommend is symbolic of that ticket.

I testify that if we are devotedly intent on returning home, we will be guided in every major decision we have to make throughout our lives—and we will enjoy the journey. Oh, let us remember, lest we forget to believe in that eternal home. I'm convinced that we do not enter this life without strong promptings that there was for each of us a significant before, and there will be a significant after. Because of the biblical account of Christ's death and resurrection, the Christian world at large believes in an afterlife. By comparison, however, very few if any understand that we were born first as spirit children, that we had to make choices before we were born on the earth, and that this mortal life is but one stage in a grand plan. Through revelations given to prophets, we as Latter-day Saints understand more concretely what Dag Hammarskjöld referred to as "coming to conscious recognition of something which we really knew all the time." . . .

The lessons we were taught in the premortal existence included the plan for our salvation. The small promptings or inklings of memory we carry into this life are like a lighthouse in the harbor that beckons us home through stormy seas.

A God in Embryo

John Taylor

Man is a dual being, possessed of body and spirit, made in the image of God, and connected with him and with eternity. He is a God in embryo and will live and progress throughout the eternal ages, if obedient to the laws of the Godhead, as the Gods progress throughout the eternal ages. . . .

. . . He is not only the son of man, but he is the son of God also. He is a God in embryo, and possesses within him a spark of that eternal flame which was struck from the blaze of God's eternal fire in the eternal world, and is placed here upon the earth that he may possess true intelligence, true light, true knowledge—that he may know himself—that he may know God—that he may know something about what he was before he came here—that he may know something about what he is destined to enjoy in the eternal worlds— that he may be fully acquainted with his origin, with his present existence, and with his future destiny—that he may know something about the strength and weakness of human nature—that he may understand the divine law, and learn to conquer his passions, and bring into subjection every principle that is at variance with the law of God—that he may understand his true relationship to God; and finally, that he may learn how to subdue, to conquer, subject all wrong, seek after, obtain, and possess every true, holy, virtuous, and heavenly principle; and, as he is only a sojourner, that he may fulfil the measure of his creation, help himself and family, be a benefit to the present and future generations, and go back to God, having accomplished the work he came here to perform. . . .

What is man? He is an immortal being. He is a part of the Deity . . . and he has come here to work out his salvation and accomplish the thing he came into existence for. We have come here to build up the kingdom of God, to establish correct principles, to teach the world righteousness, and to make millions of the human family happy—even all who will listen to the principles of eternal truth. We are here to introduce correct doctrine, to introduce correct morals, to introduce correct philosophy, to introduce correct government, and to teach men how to live and how to die—how to be happy in this world and in the world which is to come, and to lay the foundation for eternal lives in the eternal worlds.

What is man? A God, even the son of God, possessing noble aspirations, holy feelings, that may be governed by virtuous principles, possessing elevated ideas, wishing to realize everything that God has destined to submit to all his laws, to endure every kind of privation and affliction and suffering, as seeing him that is invisible, looking for a city that hath foundations, whose builder and maker is God—feeling to live for that purpose, and that alone.

This is what man is, if he lives the religion of heaven, and performs faithfully those things God has appointed him to do, that he may increase from intelligence to intelligence, and go on with that eternal progression, not only in this world, but in worlds without end.

The Doorway
of Death

Christ . . . breaketh the bands of death,

that the grave shall have no victory,

and that the sting of death should be

swallowed up in the hopes of glory.

ALMA 22:14

A Blessing in Disguise

Spencer W. Kimball

For the one who dies, life goes on and his free agency continues; and death, which seems to us such a calamity, could be a blessing in disguise. . . .

If we say that early death is a calamity, disaster, or tragedy, would it not be saying that mortality is preferable to earlier entrance into the spirit world and to eventual salvation and exaltation? if mortality be the perfect state, then death would be a frustration, but the gospel teaches us there is no tragedy in death, but only in sin: "Blessed are the dead that die in the Lord" (D&C 63:49).

We know so little. Our judgment is so limited. We judge the Lord's ways from our own narrow view. . . .

Death, then, may be the opening of the door to opportunities, including that of teaching the gospel of Christ. . . .

Everyone must die. Death is an important part of life. Of course, we are never quite ready for the change. Not knowing when it will come, we properly fight to retain our life. Yet we ought not be afraid of death. We pray for the sick, we administer to the afflicted, and we implore the Lord to heal and reduce pain, save life, and postpone death, and properly so, but not because eternity is so frightful. . . .

We knew before we were born that we were coming to the earth for bodies and experience and that we would have joys and sorrows, ease and pain, comforts and hardships, health and sickness, successes and disappointments. We knew also that after a period of life we would die. We accepted all these eventualities with a glad heart, eager to accept both the favorable and the unfavorable. We eagerly accepted the chance to come earthward even though it might be for only a day or a year. Perhaps we were not so much concerned whether we should die of disease, of accident, or of senility. We were willing to take life as it came and as we might organize and control it, and this without murmur, complaint, or unreasonable demands.

In the face of apparent tragedy we must put our trust in God, knowing that despite our limited view, his purposes will not fail. With all its troubles, life offers us the tremendous privilege to grow in knowledge and wisdom, faith and works, preparing to return and share God's glory.

From Birth to Death to Eternal Life

Robert L. Millet and
Joseph Fielding McConkie

Birth and death are inextricably intertwined, the words being defined in terms of one another. First, we are born to die and die to live. Mortal birth is tantamount to a death in regard to premortality: we die as to things as they were in order to enter the realm of mortality. In so doing, we move from "eternity" into "time." Second, having been cut off from the presence of the Father through birth in our journey from the divine presence to this fallen world and thus having died as pertaining to the things of righteousness, we are in need of a new birth. To use Paul's language, we must crucify the old man of sin and come forth in a newness of life (Romans 6:6) in order to go where God and angels dwell. Finally, we must pass beyond this veil of tears to inherit a far greater and grander existence; it is in dying that we are born unto eternal life. In mortal death we leave the realms of "time" and return to those of "eternity."

Life's starkest reality is death. Death is "a subject which strikes dread—even terror—into the hearts of most men. It is something we fear, of which we are sorely afraid, and from which most of us would flee if we could" (Bruce R. McConkie, Conference Report, October 1976, 157). It is a universal commonality, one thing which every mortal shares with every other mortal, this in spite of earthly status and accomplishments. Every man or woman is born, and every man and woman must die. All are born as helpless infants, and all are equally helpless in the face of death. Even among those who see by the lamp of gospel understanding, death is frequently viewed with fear and trembling. Joseph Smith is reported to have taught that "the Lord in his wisdom had implanted the fear of death in every person that they might cling to life and thus accomplish the designs of their Creator" (*Diary of Charles Lowell Walker* [Logan, Utah: Utah State University Press, 1980], 1:465–66). The severance of fraternal and familial ties is of all things most painful for those who remain, bringing with it an avalanche of loneliness and sorrow. Such are the feelings even of men and women of faith. He who has the panoramic vision and the broadest perspective on life and death is aware of such agonies. The God of us all has said: "Thou shalt live together in love, insomuch that thou shalt weep for the loss of them that die" (D&C 42:45).

Life's bitter winters may find us walking alone. During these cold and dark seasons of solitude, we wrap ourselves in the protective clothing of faith and its perspective and are warmed by precious memories. Thus, we move on, seeking always to view things as God views them. "Precious in the sight of the Lord," the revealed word declares, "is the death of his saints" (Psalm 116:15). "Blessed are the dead which die in the Lord," for they shall "rest from their labours; and their works do follow them" (Revelation 14:13).

A Return Home

Orson F. Whitney

We are not as good and noble in the body as we are in the spirit, and cannot be until we have subdued the body and brought it under control. We are hampered and held down by this weight of clay, and when death comes it is a glad release.

But we are not going to die. We are deathless beings. We lived before we came into this world, and we shall live after we go out of it. What we call death is not worthy the name. There is no death for the righteous. Christ died to destroy death. The change called death is but a temporary separation of the spirit from the body; and while the body goes back to mother earth, the spirit returns to God who gave it—it enters paradise, the place of departed spirits, there to await the resurrection. Yes, the day will come when spirit and body will reunite, to be no more subject to these mortal conditions, and the soul shall inherit eternal life, a fulness of joy. Such are the hopes and promises held out by the gospel.

None of our dear departed ones are dead. They have but gone before. This so-called death, when properly understood, is simply a going back home. There is a universal law requiring all things to return to whence they came and to where they belong. It is the law of restitution, spoken of by the holy prophets since the world began. This sublime lesson is taught not only in the scriptures, but in the Book of Nature. The raindrops, the moment they strike the ground, begin to trickle back to the ocean, or evaporate to the clouds from which they fell. Up from the bosom of the mighty deep and over the broad land are carried the waters that are showered upon the earth to make it green and flowery and fruitful; and when those waters have fulfilled their mission they are gathered back to their ocean reservoir. Not a drop of dew is lost.

Matter is eternal, spirit is eternal, intelligence or the light of truth is eternal; and our spirits that come from God, the moment they are born into this world begin traveling back to eternity—begin moving toward the great sea out of which they were taken! . . . No soul that believes in Jesus Christ and keeps his commandments need fear to die. It is nothing but a return home.

"Where Is Thy Sting?"

George Q. Cannon

How delightful it is to contemplate the departure of those who have been faithful, as far as their knowledge permitted, to the truth which God has revealed! There is no sting nor gloom nor inconsolable sorrow about the departure of such persons. Holy angels are around their bedside to administer unto them. The Spirit of God rests down upon them, and his messengers are near them to introduce them to those who are on the other side of the veil. . . .

Satan has power here over us to a certain extent. He can afflict us; he can tempt us; he can annoy us in many ways. These are the consequences of the Fall and for a wise purpose belong to our probation here in the flesh. But, if we listen to the Lord, if we strive to keep his commandments, if we seek to be governed by his Spirit, when death comes, Satan's power ceases. He can no more afflict or torment or tempt or annoy those who are thus faithful. His power over them ceases forever.

An Absolute Guarantee

Bruce R. McConkie

Our scriptures say: "Death hath passed upon all men, to fulfil the merciful plan of the great Creator" (2 Nephi 9:6). Where the true saints are concerned there is no sorrow in death except that which attends a temporary separation from loved ones. Birth and death are both essential steps in the unfolding drama of eternity.

We shouted for joy at the privilege of becoming mortal because without the tests of mortality there could be no eternal life. We now sing praises to the great Redeemer for the privilege of passing from this life because without death and the resurrection we could not be raised in immortal glory and gain eternal life.

When the faithful saints depart from this life, they "are received into a state of happiness, which is called paradise, a state of rest, a state of peace, where they shall rest from all their troubles and from all care, and sorrow" (Alma 40:12), and they remain in this state until the day of their resurrection. . . .

"Ye must press forward with a steadfastness in Christ," Nephi said to members of the Church, "having a perfect brightness of hope, and a love of God and of all men. Wherefore, if ye shall press forward, feasting upon the word of Christ, and endure to the end, behold, thus saith the Father: Ye shall have eternal life" (2 Nephi 31:20). That is to say—all the faithful saints, all of those who have endured to the end, depart this life with the absolute guarantee of eternal life.

There is no equivocation, no doubt, no uncertainty in our minds. Those who have been true and faithful in this life will not fall by the wayside in the life to come. If they keep their covenants here and now and depart this life firm and true in the testimony of our blessed Lord, they shall come forth with an inheritance of eternal life. . . .

. . . [W]hen the saints of God chart a course of righteousness, when they gain sure testimonies of the truth and divinity of the Lord's work, when they keep the commandments, when they overcome the world, when they put first in their lives the things of God's kingdom: when they do all these things, and then depart this life—though they have not yet become perfect—they shall nonetheless gain eternal life in our Father's kingdom; and eventually they shall be perfect as God their Father and Christ his Son are perfect.

Jesus' Example

Spencer W. Kimball

As Jesus' spirit left his body hanging on the cross and later lying in the tomb, so shall our spirits eventually leave our bodies lying lifeless. As Jesus preached to spirits in the spirit world in his spiritual state, so shall our spirits continue active and expand and develop. As Jesus appeared in the garden a resurrected soul, so shall each of us come forth a perfect immortal with every organ perfect, every limb intact, with every injury or deformity restored and put right; with the infirmities of mortality replaced with strength and vigor and power and beauty of virile maturity.

The meaning of death has not changed. It releases a spirit for growth and development and places a body in the repair shop of Mother Earth, there to be recast, remolded into a perfect body, an immortal glorious temple, clean, whole, perfected, and ready for its occupant for eternity.

A Link in a Living Chain

George Q. Cannon

We are in reality, while in this mortality, aliens and strangers. We are far distant from our father's house, living in a cold world far removed from those affections which we doubtless have experienced in the spirit world, and which we will again enjoy, if we are faithful to the trust reposed in us on the earth.

. . . How happy will be the meeting of the faithful with their Father in Heaven. Our old affections, of which we know but little at this time, will be revived, and we shall enjoy ourselves, with a joy that to us is inexpressible now.

It is right that the ties should be strengthened between us and the spirit world. Every one who departs from this mortal state of existence only adds another link to the chain of connection—another tie to draw us nearer to our Father and God, and to those intelligences which dwell in his presence. . . . Those of us who have lost children, brothers and sisters and parents, feel an increased interest in the spirit world; the ties between such and the spirit world have become binding, and we can contemplate, if not with delight, at least with no great sorrow, our removal from this state of existence to the next. . . .

God has given us the testimony of his Spirit, which bears witness to our spirits that we shall again be united with our departed friends after death. Our mortal tabernacles may sleep, but our spirits are eternal, and, if faithful here, we shall enjoy an immortality in the presence of God that will amply reward us for all that we may suffer on earth.

The State of the Soul

Joseph F. Smith

While we are in mortality we are clogged, and we see as through a glass darkly, we see only in part, and it is difficult for us to comprehend the smallest things with which we are associated. But when we put on immortality, our condition will be very different, for we ascend into an enlarged sphere; although we shall not become perfect immediately after our departure from the body, for the spirit without the body is not perfect, and the body without the spirit is dead.

The disembodied spirit during the interval [between] the death of the body and its resurrection from the grave is not perfect, hence it is not prepared to enter into the exaltation of the celestial kingdom; but it has the privilege of soaring in the midst of immortal beings, and of enjoying, to a certain extent, the presence of God, not the fulness of his glory, not the fulness of the reward which we are seeking and which we are destined to receive, if found faithful to the law of the celestial kingdom, but only in part.

The righteous spirit that departs from this earth is assigned its place in the paradise of God; it has its privileges and honors which are in point of excellency, far above and beyond human comprehension; and in this sphere of action, enjoying this partial reward for its righteous conduct on the earth, it continues its labors, and in this respect is very different from the state of the body from which it is released. For while the body sleeps and decays, the spirit . . . is born again into the spirit world, returning there from the mission it has been performing in this state of probation, having been absent a few years from father, mother, kindred, friends, neighbors, and from all that was dear; it has returned nearer to the home circle, to old associations and scenes, much in the same way as a man who comes home from a foreign mission, to join again his family and friends and enjoy the pleasures and comforts of home.

This is the condition . . . of every one who has been faithful to virtue and purity, while traveling here below; but more especially of those who while here had the privilege of obeying the gospel, and who lived true and faithful to its covenants. Instead of continuing here among the things of time, surrounded as we are with the weaknesses of a fallen world, and subject to earthly cares and sorrows, they are freed from them to enter a state of joy, glory and exaltation; not a fulness of any one of them but to await the morning of the resurrection of the just, to come forth from the grave to redeem the body, and to be reunited with it and thus become a living soul, an immortal being, never more to die. Having accomplished its work, having gone through its earthly probation, and having fulfilled its mission here below, it is then prepared for the knowledge and glory and exaltation of the celestial kingdom.

This Jesus did; and he is our forerunner, he is our exemplar. The path which he marked out we have to walk, if we ever expect to dwell and be crowned with him in his kingdom. We must obey and put our trust in him, knowing that he is the Savior of the world.

To Exist Eternally

Brigham Young

The gospel of life and salvation reveals to each individual who receives it that this world is only a place of temporary duration, existence, trials, &c. Its present fashion and uses are but for a few days, while we were created to exist eternally. . . . We understand that when we are unclothed in this present state, then we are prepared to be clothed upon with immortality—that when we put off these bodies we put on immortality. These bodies will return to dust, but our hope and faith are that we will receive these bodies again from the elements—that we will receive the very organization that we have here, and that, if we are faithful to the principles of freedom, we shall then be prepared to endure eternally.

. . . The inhabitants of the earth are continually coming and going. This is not our abiding place. All can see naturally, if they would but observe the facts before them, that this world is but of short duration to them. They appear here infants, pass through childhood and youth to middle age, and if they live to a good old age, it is but a short time, and then they must go. . . .

This is only our place of temporary existence. We cannot live here always with our bodies full of pain and subject to decay. Deprive us of food and we die; deprive us of water, and after a short time we die; deprive us of air, and we live but a few moments. We all know that this is not the state for us to live in and endure to eternity. Our eyes are looking beyond this sphere of action, and I trust that we are laying the foundation to endure eternally. If we do, we must be the friends of God—the friends of the principles of life and salvation; and we must adhere to those principles and shape our lives according to them, or else we lay the foundation for our own destruction.

An Actual Death, a Literal Resurrection

James E. Talmage

The Church of Jesus Christ of Latter-day Saints teaches the doctrine of a literal resurrection, an actual reunion of the spirits of the dead and the tabernacles with which they were clothed during mortal probation. . . .

The return of spring after the death-like sleep of winter; the passing of the crawling caterpillar into the corpse-like chrysalis, and the subsequent emergence of the winged butterfly; the coming forth of a living bird from the tomb-like recess of the egg—these and other natural processes of development have been used as illustrative of the resurrection. Each of them falls short, for in no instance of such awakening has there been actual death. If the tree die it will not resume its leafage with the return of the sun; if the pupa within the chrysalis, or the life-germ within the egg be killed, no butterfly or bird will emerge. . . .

The body, deserted by its immortal tenant, is literally dead; it resolves itself into its natural components, and its substance enters again upon the round of universal circulation of matter. Yet the resurrection from the dead is assured; the faith of those who trust in the word of revealed truth will be vindicated, and the divine decree will be carried into full effect.

"When the Voice Calls for the Dead"

Joseph Smith

Those who have died in Jesus Christ may expect to enter into all that fruition of joy when they come forth, which they possessed or anticipated here.

So plain was the vision, that I actually saw men, before they had ascended from the tomb, as though they were getting up slowly. They took each other by the hand and said to each other, "My father, my son, my mother, my daughter, my brother, my sister." And when the voice calls for the dead to arise, suppose I am laid by the side of my father, what would be the first joy of my heart? To meet my father, my mother, my brother, my sister; and when they are by my side, I embrace them and they me. . . .

All your losses will be made up to you in the resurrection, provided you continue faithful. By the vision of the Almighty I have seen it.

. . . If I have no expectation of seeing my father, mother, brothers, sisters and friends again, my heart would burst in a moment, and I should go down to my grave.

The expectation of seeing my friends in the morning of the resurrection cheers my soul and makes me bear up against the evils of life. It is like their taking a long journey, and on their return we meet them with increased joy.

All Will Be Resurrected

J. Reuben Clark Jr.

This is the glorious message that comes from out the ministry of Christ—by the fall of Adam, all die, but by the atonement of Christ, all shall again live—every man, woman, and child born to this earth shall in due time rise from the grave to everlasting life. . . .

From the time of the Fall, men knew of the atoning sacrifice that would be offered by the Only Begotten, that it would bring to all mankind a redemption from the mortal death brought into the world by Adam.

The day of the transgression of Adam brought his separation from the Father, with whom, before that day, he had walked and talked—this separation was a spiritual death. But Adam's transgression also brought mortality and the death of the body. Thus all men must die, and, as Adam left them when he passed on, they must sleep forever.

But that was not God's plan set up at the beginning. That plan provided that his children should come to earth, take on mortal bodies, and, if they lived his laws and kept his commandments, they should "have glory added upon their heads for ever and ever" in the life hereafter (Abraham 3:26).

So there must be a rising from the dead in order that the mortal body and the spirit might be reunited to form the soul, even as God had planned.

To bring this about, Christ was born, ministered, died, and was resurrected, and being resurrected, his body and spirit were again reunited, for he declared to his disciples, in the evening of the day of his resurrection, that he was not a spirit, but a being of "flesh and bones" (Luke 24:39).

This redemption from death, this resurrection of the mortal body, is to come to all men who have ever lived, from the beginning till the end, to those who heard the truth while living and to those who have died without the truth. Resurrection from the dead is humanity-wide, none, even the most depraved, lose this blessing. . . .

But while every mortal shall be raised from the dead through the atonement of Christ, we shall not all rise equal in all things, any more than we are all equal, spiritually and intellectually in mortality. Jesus said . . . men are to come forth "they that have done good, unto the resurrection of life; and they that have done evil, unto the resurrection of damnation" (John 5:29). . . . According to their deeds, men will rise to celestial glory, to terrestrial glory, or to telestial glory, or to a resurrection without glory, depending upon the kind of lives they lived while on the earth. Blessed are they who rise to a celestial glory, for they shall live with the Father. Sad will be they who rise to no glory, for they shall not live with the Father.

An Eternal Identity

Joseph F. Smith

We distinctly believe that Jesus Christ himself is the true, and only true type of the resurrection of men from death unto life. We believe there is no other form of resurrection from death to life; that as he rose, and as he preserved his identity, even to the scars of the wounds in his hands and feet and side, that he could prove himself to those that were skeptical of the possibility of rising from the dead, that he was indeed himself, the Lord crucified, buried in the tomb, and raised again from death to life.

So it will be with you and with every son and daughter of Adam born into the world. You will not lose your identity any more than Christ did. You will be brought forth from death to life again, just as sure as Christ was brought forth from death to life again . . . —therefore, in the same manner in which Christ has been raised, so will life, and the resurrection from death to life again, come upon all who have descended from our first parents. The death that came into the world by Adam's transgression has been conquered, and its terror vanquished by the power and righteousness of the Son of God. . . .

Why did he teach us the principle of eternal union of man and wife? Because God knew that we were his children here, to remain his children forever and ever, and that we were just as truly individuals, and that our individuality was . . . identical [to] that of the Son of God, and would therefore continue so worlds without end. So that the man receiving his wife by the power of God, for time and for all eternity, would have the right to claim her and she to claim her husband in the world to come. Neither would be changed, except from mortality to immortality, neither would be other than himself or herself; but they will have their identity in the world to come, precisely as they exercise their individuality and enjoy their identity here. God has revealed this principle . . . ; and we are willing to stand by it; and our children, and our children's children after us to the latest generation, will abide in this truth, for it is founded on revelation from God.

An Eternity
of Glory

And I know that he will raise me up

at the last day, to dwell with him in glory;

yea, and I will praise him forever.

ALMA 36:28

His Work and His Glory

Stephen E. Robinson

According to John, "God is love" (1 John 4:8, 16). And how exactly is this love expressed? What does God *do*? He tells us himself in the Pearl of Great Price: "This is my work and my glory—to bring to pass the immortality and eternal life of man" (Moses 1:39). God's work is *us!* What he does for a living is to make us wretched humans be more, be better, be greater.

It is vital we understand that this scripture doesn't apply only to God's celestial children but to *all* of them. The many mansions in our Father's house include the terrestrial and telestial kingdoms as well as the celestial. They are all kingdoms of *glory*. It isn't just his obedient children who are part of God's work and glory and for whom he labors; it is all of them who will be redeemed from the devil and raised to any degree of glory whatever (see, for example, D&C 76:42–43, 85, 88–89).

In other words, God improves *everybody;* he blesses everyone and everything he touches; it is his nature to raise and to bless. He has raised us from whatever we were before we were spirits to make us his spirit children. He has given those of his children who would allow it physical bodies. And in the resurrection he will give us eternal glory to the degree that we have allowed it. God tries to give all his children celestial glory, but if we resist that, he tries to give us terrestrial glory. And if we resist that, he tries to give us telestial glory.

It is his work to maximize our eternal condition, to get us the best deal in eternity that he can—it's what he does for a living. Naturally, he wants to give all of us everything, but of course most of us resist him—so he gives us what he can. It's his job—his "work"; and it's what makes him great—his "glory." Saving us and improving us is what he's all about.

"How Will You Spend Eternity?"

Orson F. Whitney

I picked up a card on a railroad train one day, a card on which was printed this question: *"Where do you expect to spend eternity?"* A very interesting query, and a very difficult one for some people to answer. But "Mormonism" answers it, and it is the only religion that can answer it consistently. "Mormonism" says that when we pass out of the body we are in the spirit world, and will remain there, the righteous resting from their labors—not in idleness, but in doing, working without weariness, without pain, while awaiting a glorious resurrection, when they are to have the privilege of coming back to spend their time on this planet, when it is celestialized and converted into a heaven.

About the time that I picked up that card and read the question thereon, a similar question was going the rounds of the religious magazines. Thus: *"How do you expect to spend eternity?"* This question caused quite a discussion. One reverend gentleman answered it in these words: "How do I expect to spend eternity? I expect to spend the first million years gazing upon the face of the Savior. And then," he added, somewhat facetiously, "I might take a sidelong glance at my wife."

Poor lone woman, waiting a million years for that sidelong glance! Is it not plain that her loving husband did not know how to answer the question? If he had known he would have told, and made himself famous; but he did not know, and so passed it off as a joke. But it is no joke, this problem of life and death and resurrection and the hereafter. It is a solemn and sublime reality.

But assuming that he was serious and really meant what he said, let us consider for a moment the gentleman's reply. Does any sane man or woman believe that an all-wise God would create an earth like this, and place his children upon it to [develop their abilities] . . . , and then whisk them away to some distant part of the universe, some world "beyond the bounds of time and space," where they would sit down and twiddle their thumbs and stare somebody out of countenance for a million years? Is it reasonable? Is it sensible?

How would a Latter-day Saint answer such a question? One who understands his religion—an intelligent, thoughtful Latter-day Saint, if asked: "How do you expect to spend eternity?" would be very apt to reply: "I expect to spend it in doing there the things I have learned to do here." That is common sense. It is logical, economical. Else were this all wasted time.

No, we are not going to sit down through all eternity and gaze upon the face of the Savior. I don't believe he would want anyone to look at him that long. It would be bad manners. We shall do in eternity the things we have learned to do in time, but we will do them better there than here. We will be better fathers and mothers, better husbands and wives, better in every way; and every faculty exercised and developed here, will find full play and employment in the Great Hereafter. . . .

> "Then shall I see and hear and know
> All I desired and wished below,
> And every power find sweet employ
> In that eternal world of joy."

Eternal Life Is God's Life

Bruce R. McConkie

Immortality is one thing, eternal life another. Immortality is to live forever in a resurrected state; it is to have a tangible body of flesh and bones. After the judgment, immortal beings are assigned their places in the celestial, terrestrial, and telestial kingdoms. Eternal life is the name of the kind of life possessed by the Eternal One, by the Eternal Father. It is reserved for those immortal beings who gain an inheritance in the highest heaven of the celestial realm.

Both immortality and eternal life come because of the Atonement; both are part of the gospel. Immortality is for all men, both the righteous and the wicked; eternal life is for those who believe and obey the whole law of the whole gospel. . . . Immortality is the ransom from temporal death; eternal life is the ransom from spiritual death. Both come by the grace of God. One comes as a free gift; the other is earned by obedience to the laws and ordinances of the gospel.

The whole purpose of the plan of salvation is to provide immortality for all men and to make eternal life available for those who overcome the world and qualify for such a high exaltation. "For behold, this is my work and my glory," saith God, "to bring to pass the immortality and eternal life of man" (Moses 1:39). This is accomplished through the redemption of Christ, by virtue of which all men are "raised in immortality," thus being redeemed from the temporal fall, and by virtue of which the saints are "raised [also] unto eternal life," thus being "redeemed from their spiritual fall" (D&C 29:43–44).

Salvation is in Christ. Immortality comes through him; his resurrection brings to pass the resurrection of all men. Eternal life is his gift to those whose sins he has borne. "I am the resurrection, and the life," he said. Both immortality and eternal life come because of [his] atoning sacrifice. "He that believeth in me, though he were dead, yet shall he live." Temporal death and spiritual death are both swallowed up in Christ. "And whosoever liveth and believeth in me shall never die" (John 11:25–26). Those who are alive in Christ because they have the companionship of the Holy Spirit shall never die. They are alive spiritually in this sphere, and they shall have eternal life in the realms ahead. . . .

Immortality is for all men; eternal life is for a favored few. Eternal life is available to all, for God is no respecter of persons, but few will pay the price in service, in obedience, and in personal righteousness to gain so great a gift. In its very nature and by definition, eternal life consists of two things: (1) the continuation of the family unit in eternity, and (2) receiving the fulness of the glory and power of the Father.

God also has all power, all might, and all dominion. He knows all things, has all wisdom, and is the embodiment of all truth. Those who receive a like state of glory and exaltation become like him; they become one with the Father and the Son. They are the ones of whom Jesus said: "Ye shall be even as I am, and I am even as the Father; and the Father and I are one" (3 Nephi 28:10).

What Would You Give?

Mark E. Petersen

Where do you want to spend eternity? Where would you like your family to spend eternity?

If you knew that by living the gospel you may have celestial glory rather than a lesser one, would it not be worth the effort to obtain it?

Who would be satisfied with the subdued twinkle of a star if he could enjoy the brilliance of the sun?

Who would be content with the reflected light of the moon if he could have the radiance of the sun?

Who would exchange the privilege of becoming like God for the very questionable and temporary advantages of this world?

Who in his right mind would prefer the corruptions of the flesh, the sensual pleasures, and the false excitement of sin, rather than the opportunity of becoming like God, rather than having inspired intelligence, or of some day wielding some of the powers that God uses as he walks in his majesty?

Which of us would sell his birthright for a mess of pottage?

Unequaled Blessings

Brigham Young

Suppose it possible that you have the privilege of securing to yourselves eternal life—to live and enjoy these blessings forever; you will say this is the greatest blessing that can be bestowed upon you, to live forever and enjoy the society of wives, children, and children's children, to a thousand generations, and forever; also the society of brethren, sisters, neighbors, and associates, and to possess all you can ask for to make you happy and comfortable. What blessing is equal to this? What blessing is equal to the continuation of life— to the continuation of our organizations?

The Lord has blessed us with the ability to enjoy an eternal life with the Gods, and this is pronounced the greatest gift of God. The gift of eternal life, without a posterity, to become an angel, is one of the greatest gifts bestowed; yet the Lord has bestowed on us the privilege of becoming fathers of lives. What is a father of lives, as mentioned in the scriptures? A man who has a posterity to an eternal continuance. That is the blessing Abraham received, and it perfectly satisfied his soul. He obtained the promise that he should be the father of lives. In comparison with this, what did Abraham care about machinery, railroads, and other great mechanical productions? We have the privilege of becoming fathers of lives to all eternity and of existing in the presence of God. Is not this worthy of our living in righteousness and complete obedience to the commandments of God?

Claim Your Crown

Spencer W. Kimball

You are heirs to great fortunes, for eternal life is the greatest gift.

What will you do with it? You are entitled to a kingdom or a queendom. You are princesses and princes. Do you prize your inheritance? Will you abdicate and relinquish your heavenly rights to all that is your due? Do you but realize what the Lord has in store for you? Do you know what you could discard in a moment of carelessness and heedlessness? The Lord told his servants:

"Eye hath not seen, nor ear heard, neither have entered into the heart of man, the things which God hath prepared for them that love him" (1 Corinthians 2:9).

The king's highway—the royal road to eternal joys and exaltation—is a hard road, full of sacrifices and restrictions and hard work. The way is narrow, but it is straight, well-marked, and strongly-beamed. But if you get off course, the dot and dash tapping gets dimmer and fainter till it fades out entirely.

The permanent kingdom is yours, not for the asking, but for the earning.

Will you abdicate it? That is much easier than to claim it. Will you . . . voluntarily renounce the throne? And through carelessness and heedlessness voluntarily relinquish your right to this powerful and blessed privilege? Will you forfeit your crown? Will you turn over your scepter to another? It follows easily. To do so, you need only to forget the Lord, ignore his commandments, become critical or bitter or inactive. Other things follow in turn, and your kingship and queenship are in jeopardy! . . .

What are you going to do? . . .

O, my beloved [friends], I pray you, . . . plan your course, chart your way, live righteously always, listen to your leaders, read the scriptures, think sanely, pray much and often, earn your eternal throne, claim your crown, hold tightly the scepter, keep your inheritance inviolate.

May you . . . never abdicate your possible thrones, but become priests and kings, queens and priestesses of the most high throughout eternity.

The Lord's Invitation

Lorenzo Snow

Through a continual course of progression, our Heavenly Father has received exaltation and glory, and he points us out the same path; and inasmuch as he is clothed with power, authority, and glory, he says, "Walk ye up and come in possession of the same glory and happiness that I possess."

In the gospel those things have been made manifest unto us, and we are perfectly assured that, inasmuch as we are faithful, we shall eventually come in possession of everything that the mind of man can conceive of—everything that heart can desire.

Well, then, in the midst of poverty and deprivations, or in the midst of comforts and conveniences, still these hopes are the secret springs of our joys. We see that our Heavenly Father does provide us with everything we need; we see that we are in the sure path to come in possession of those richer blessings that are promised; and nothing in this world can, or ever will, place an impediment in our way to prevent us from receiving those blessings.

Is not our liberty, our comfort in the everlasting gospel, the assurance that we shall receive all the reward that is made sure to the faithful children of God? Then where is the man that is not willing to set fire to his substance—that is not willing to yield everything for the salvation of himself and the people, if that be the principle upon which salvation is to be obtained?

Let a man have the visions of the Almighty unfolded to

his view and see in yonder heavens the government of the eternal worlds—let him see the liberty and joy that are to be participated in, and let him see that the gospel gives all to this man, and he is willing in his heart and in his feelings to yield everything to the will of God, that he may come in possession of those things. Will such a man pursue a course that will eventually throw him out of the kingdom? Will he give up those blessings and those prospects for a little comfort, or for a little of this world's goods, or to enjoy the comforts of this life for a season?

Where is there cause to mourn? Where is there cause for the saints to wear long faces? Where is there cause for weeping or repining? There is none; but it is life or death that is set before us. Principalities and powers are ours, if we continue faithful; sorrow and banishment, if we disregard the gospel.

Blessed Are God's Children

LeGrand Richards

[My wife] and I were filling a mission together over in Holland when we had a little girl born to us, and after we had been home a few years she passed away. When she was born, my wife has told me over and over again that she felt she saw an angel bring that spirit to her. And yet she is gone. . . .

When I think of this little one that we laid away when she was three-and-a-half years old, I thank God I have the faith to believe that God reigns in the heavens above and in the earth beneath and that this little one will ultimately enter into her glory and be equal to any of her four sisters who have tarried here upon this earth and raised their families. I thank God for the statement of the Apostle Paul when he said that "if in this life only we have hope in Christ, we are of all men most miserable" (1 Corinthians 15:19). In this brief period of mortality, it would not be possible for God to accomplish for all of his children all that he has in mind for them, the ones that are true and faithful. . . .

All that God has ultimately planned for his children who are faithful and true shall come to them in his own due time.

"Formed for Eternity"

Joseph F. Smith

We live for time and for eternity. We form associations and relations for time and all eternity. Our affections and our desires are found fitted and prepared to endure not only throughout the temporal or mortal life, but through all eternity. Who are there besides the Latter-day Saints who contemplate the thought that beyond the grave we will continue in the family organization? the father, the mother, the children recognizing each other in the relations which they owe to each other and in which they stand to each other? this family organization being a unit in the great and perfect organization of God's work, and all destined to continue throughout time and eternity?

We are living for eternity and not merely for the moment. Death does not part us from one another, if we have entered into sacred relationships with each other by virtue of the authority that God has revealed to the children of men. Our relationships are formed for eternity. We are immortal beings, and we are looking forward to the growth that is to be attained in an exalted life after we have proved ourselves faithful and true to the covenants that we have entered into here, and then we will receive a fulness of joy.

Thirty-Five Million Years

LeGrand Richards

When my wife and I had been married thirty-five years, I said [to her], "What do you think we will be doing in thirty-five million years from today?"

She said, "Where did you get that crazy idea? It makes me tired to think of it!"

I said, "Well, you believe in eternal life, don't you?" I said, "We are told that time is measured only to man, that with God there isn't such a thing as time. It is one eternal round." (The Prophet Joseph illustrated this by taking a ring. He said, "When you cut it, there is a beginning and there is an end, but as long as you don't cut it, there is no beginning and there is no end.") Then I said, "Now, . . . if you believe that, you and I ought to be pretty well acquainted with each other in thirty-five million years from today."

"Adapted to the Highest Glories"

Parley P. Pratt

When man, and the planet on which he lives, with all its fullness, shall have completed all their series of progressive changes, so as to be adapted to the highest glories of which their several characters and species are capable, then, the whole will be annexed to, or numbered with the eternal heavens, and will there fulfill their eternal rounds. . . .

Worlds are mansions for the home of intelligences.

Intelligences exist in order to enjoy.

Joy, in its fullness, depends on certain principles, namedly, Life Eternal, Love Eternal, Peace Eternal, Wealth Eternal. . . .

Without the first, enjoyment lacks durability.

Without the second, it can hardly be said to exist.

Without the third, it would not be secure.

Without the fourth, it must be limited. . . .

. . . Eternal man in possession of eternal worlds, in all their variety and fullness, will eat, drink, think, converse, associate, assemble, disperse, go, come, possess, . . . love and enjoy. He will increase in riches, . . . majesty, and dominion in worlds without end. . . .

Socrates, Plato, Confucius, and many other philosophers and divines have written largely on the immortality of the *soul* or spirit of man.

Some of these have suffered, with joy and cheerfulness,

imprisonment, torture, and even death, with only this limited view of eternal existence.

Could these martyrs to a portion of truth so limited, and yet so full of hope and consolation, have handled immortal flesh and bones in the persons of Enoch or Elijah translated, or of Jesus raised from the dead; could they have learned from their sacred lips, and realized the full import of that joyful sentence—*"Behold! I make all things new"*; could they have contemplated eternal worlds of matter in all its elements and forms of animal life, indissoluble and everlasting; could they have beheld eternal man, moving in the majesty of God, amid the planetary systems, grasping the knowledge of universal nature, and with an intellect enlightened by the experience and observations of thousands and even millions of years; could they have had a glimpse of all this, and heard the promise—*"There shall be no more death,"* issuing from the fountain of truth, prompted by infinite benevolence and charity, re-echoing amid the starry worlds, reaching down to earth, vibrating with a thrill of joy, all the myriads of animated nature, penetrating the gloomy vaults of death and the prisons of the spirit world, with a ray of hope, and causing to spring afresh, the well-springs of life, and joy and love, even in the lonely dungeons of despair! O! how would their bosoms have reverberated with unutterable joy and triumph.

The Emperor's Child

Lorenzo Snow

How is it that God proposes to confer this mighty honor upon us and to raise us to this condition of glory and exaltation? Who are we that God should do all this for us? Why, we are just beginning to find out that we are the offspring of God, born with the same faculties and powers as he possesses, capable of enlargement through the experience that we are now passing through in our second estate.

Let me illustrate. Here is an emperor sitting upon his throne, governing and controlling his empire wisely and properly. He has an infant son that sits upon the knee of its mother. That son he proposes to one day set upon his throne, to govern and control his empire. Here is that infant, perfectly helpless, not knowing how to sustain its own life, not able to walk alone, without any knowledge; and here is this mighty emperor sitting upon his throne and governing his vast empire. Who would believe that he could raise that infant up to such a condition as to make it suitable to be placed on his throne? No one would, unless he had seen such things accomplished in his experience, seen the infant develop into boyhood, and then to manhood, possessing all the powers, faculties and possibilities of its father.

Now, we are the sons and daughters of God. He has begotten us in his own image. He has given us faculties and powers that are capable of enlargement until his fulness is reached which he has promised—until we shall sit upon thrones, governing and controlling our posterity from eternity to eternity, and increasing eternally. . . .

God has pointed out the results of traveling upon this road of glory and exaltation, and the promises are sure. The Lord knew precisely what he could do. He knew what materials he had to operate with, and he knew just what he said. If we do the part that he has assigned unto us and keep our second estate, we shall be sure to realize these promises in every particular, and more than you and I can possibly comprehend.

Joint Heirs with Christ

Robert L. Millet

Jesus Christ has offered us the privilege of supping with him and his Father at the family table, of enjoying full family status and benefits with him. In short, he has offered us adoption as sons and daughters. "God sent forth his Son, made of a woman, made under the law, to redeem them that were under the law, that we might receive the adoption of sons. And because ye are sons, God hath sent forth the Spirit of his Son into your hearts, crying, Abba, Father. Wherefore thou art no more a servant, but a son; and if a son, then an heir of God through Christ" (Galatians 4:4–7).

It was never intended that men and women remain children forever, even children of Jesus Christ. After we have received the appropriate ordinances and entered into sacred covenants; after we have chosen to forsake evil, have begun to have dross and iniquity burned out of our souls as though by fire, have become alive to the things of the Spirit and thus been born again; after we have taken the name of Christ and become his sons and daughters by covenant—after such growth, we may yet qualify for greater family blessings: We may become sons and daughters of God the Father and thus joint heirs with Christ to all the Father has. We are not joint heirs with Christ as his children. Through the ordinances of the temple, particularly eternal marriage, we qualify to inherit, receive, and possess equally with Christ. He is the Firstborn and is entitled to all the blessings of the Firstborn.

Through his mercy and grace, he offers to raise us up to possess equally with him the blessings of the Firstborn. . . .

Our Father in Heaven has sent us into the world and essentially implanted the words into our souls: "Remember who you are, and act accordingly." We are his spirit sons and daughters. We have the opportunity to receive forgiveness of sin and reconciliation with his royal family through the atonement of Jesus Christ. We have the privilege of being children of the covenant, sons and daughters of Abraham, Isaac, and Jacob. And we have the power through Christ and through the ordinances of the temple to grow in spiritual grace until we become the sons and daughters of God the Father and joint heirs with him who is the Firstborn. God is literally our Father, and the most important unit in time and eternity is the family. . . . As new creatures alive in Christ, we have come back home. The Gods wait patiently to welcome us.

The Spark of Divinity

George Q. Cannon

It is a glorious thing . . . to know that our religion is true and given us from God and that in obedience to it we may attain to the exalted position occupied by him and our Lord and Savior Jesus Christ. . . . We are of the race of God, the sons and daughters of a King. What monarch's children do not hope and look forward to sovereignty? May we, who are the offspring of the Almighty King, not hope for crowns and kingdoms in eternity?

Some believe our eternal destiny is to sit upon clouds, thrum harps and sing forever. What an occupation! What a monotony! No matter how sweet this music might be it would become very wearisome if extended so long. But such is not our destiny. Our mission hereafter is to perpetuate and continue the work of our Father and our God, to perpetuate our species and to create worlds from the elements by which we are surrounded.

Go out at night and behold the starry firmament. The millions of shining orbs we see are the work of God—worlds created and peopled by the Almighty. Such works are for us to do. Eternity is before us, and every man and every woman will find ample room for the exercise of every faculty he or she may possess. How glorious to think that we have the spark of divinity within us.

Something of God in Us

Hugh B. Brown

You should always remember that you are here for a purpose, that you have a life's mission assigned to you by your Father, that because he is your Father, there is something of him in you, and you can, by diligence and vigilance and purity of life, become like him from whom you came.

Palm trees do not grow from acorns. The acorn can, under proper conditions, grow into the oak because the oak is involved in the acorn. Only that which is involved can evolve and, as you are the sons of God, he is somehow involved in you, and you can evolve by obedience to law into something like him—evolve into Godhood because God, being your Father, is involved in you. This is one of the most profound and inspiring truths in the world, that man is literally a son of God. He, the King of Kings, is your Father, and you must be loyal to the royal that is in you.

A Heavenly Mandate

Tad R. Callister

Paul knew our potential as offspring of God, for while speaking to the Romans he declared, "The Spirit itself beareth witness with our spirit, that we are the children of God: and if children, then heirs; heirs of God, and joint-heirs with Christ" (Romans 8:16–17)—not subordinate heirs, not junior, not contingent, but joint, equal heirs with Christ, to share in all that he shall receive. President Joseph F. Smith understood the significance of this scripture, for he observed, "The grand object of our coming to this earth is that we may become like Christ, for if we are not like him, we cannot become the sons of God, and be joint heirs with Christ" (*Gospel Doctrine*, 18). John the Revelator saw in vision how all-inclusive this inheritance might be, even for a struggling mortal: "He that overcometh shall inherit all things; and I will be his God, and he shall be my son" (Revelation 21:7). There are no qualifiers here. The Lord does not promise "some things" or even "many things," but rather "all things." Timothy knew of this possibility. Paul promised him, "If we suffer, we shall also reign with him" (2 Timothy 2:12). The word *reign* suggests a kingdom, a dominion over which we will have rule. The words *reign with him* suggest a position of *like* power and rule. The Lord was most specific on this issue: "He [God] makes them equal in power, and in might, and in dominion" (D&C 76:95). Again and again, the message is clear and consistent.

Is it any wonder that Paul should write to the saints of

Philippi, "I press toward the mark for the prize of the high calling of God in Christ Jesus" (Philippians 3:14)? Paul, who understood this doctrine, was striving for the prize of godhood. He then extended this universal invitation to all saints, "Let us therefore, as many as be perfect, be thus minded" (Philippians 3:15). . . . Speaking to the saints of Philippi, he said, "Let this mind be in you, which was also in Christ Jesus: who, being in the form of God, *thought it not robbery to be equal with God*" (Philippians 2:5–6; emphasis added). The Savior knew that for him to be a god would not rob God of his divinity. Paul carries this one step further. He suggests that each of us should view these things as Jesus did, for if we do, we will also know that it is possible for us to become like God without robbing him of his divinity. . . . Godhood for man does not diminish God's status; to the contrary, it elevates it by producing more intelligent, more sensitive, more respectful saints who have enlarged capacities to understand, honor, and worship him.

The Savior's soul-stirring and thought-provoking injunction to "be ye therefore perfect" (Matthew 5:48) was more than the sounding of brass or tinkling of cymbals. It was a heavenly mandate to rise up to our full potential and become like God our Father.

The Purpose for Our Creation

Brigham Young

Man is made an agent to himself before his God; he is organized for the express purpose that he may become like his master. You recollect one of the apostle's sayings, that when we see Him, we shall be like Him; and again, we shall become Gods, even the sons of God (1 John 3:2; D&C 76:58). . . .

. . . The Lord created you and me for the purpose of becoming Gods like himself, when we have been proved in our present capacity and been faithful with all things he puts into our possession. We are created, we are born for the express purpose of growing up from the low estate of manhood, to become Gods like unto our Father in heaven. That is the truth about it, just as it is. The Lord has organized mankind for the express purpose of increasing in that intelligence and truth, which is with God, until he is capable of creating worlds on worlds and becoming Gods, even the sons of God.

How many will become thus privileged? Those who honor the Father and the Son; those who receive the Holy Ghost, and magnify their calling, and are found pure and holy; they shall be crowned in the presence of the Father and the Son. Who else? Not anybody. . . . [Only these shall] go into the celestial kingdom, into the presence of the Father and the Son, and . . . be made an heir to his kingdom, and all his glory, and be crowned with crowns of glory, immortality, and eternal lives.

"Drink the Heavenly Draught, and Live"

*Robert L. Millet and
Joseph Fielding McConkie*

The gospel has been restored, the heavens have been opened, the veil has been rent, and the great God, the Father of us all, has been revealed. The secret of the ages has been made known—God is an exalted man! We are in reality his children and thus of the lineage of the Gods. Our spirits were begotten of heavenly parents, our mortal bodies bear God's image and likeness, and our destiny is to become as he is. Let then the heavens ring with these singular truths: God is our Father! We are his children! We can become as he is. . . .

. . . Such is within the reach of all who will pay the price. This marvelous accomplishment—the ability to be even as our exalted Sire—is the consummation of that process of spiritual development which begins in premortality, continues with an accelerated pace while in the flesh, and moves on to realization in the worlds beyond the grave. . . .

. . . Man is of the same species as God, and as such has the capacity, through extended righteousness and faith, to rise to the station of a god. Our God is not possessive of godhood, but is an exalted Father who pleads with his posterity with tender regard to follow the path he has already trod, a path which leads not only to the ultimate in joy and happiness, but also to a complete realization of all it was intended for man to become. The cup with its draught of possibilities beyond the grave runneth over, a cup extended to the obedient. The beckoning call of the Lord is, "Drink, then, the heavenly draught, and live!"

"Sit with Me in My Throne"

Tad R. Callister

We may not control our temporal setbacks, but we always, always, always control our spiritual destiny. Every temporal tragedy may be countered with a spiritual victory—and the ultimate victory is godhood. In the last analysis, through his grace, God has permitted us to define our own divine destiny.

. . . Almost two thousand years ago the Lord made this astounding promise to John the Revelator: "To him that overcometh will I grant *to sit with me in my throne*, even as I also overcame, and am set down with my Father in his throne" (Revelation 3:21; emphasis added). What was that throne? Nothing less than the throne of God. . . .

Some might ask, What difference does it make if I really understand this principle of godhood? Elder McConkie wrote, "No doctrine is more basic, no doctrine embraces a greater incentive to personal righteousness . . . as does the wondrous concept that man can be as his Maker" (*Promised Messiah*, 133). As we better understand this lofty goal, our level of confidence and motivation is greatly heightened. How could we not have increased faith in God and in ourselves by knowing he had planted within our souls the seeds of godhood?

The Atonement is the sun, water, and soil that nourish those seeds. It is the eternal power so essential to our growth. That is what John Taylor taught: "It is for the exaltation of man to this state of superior intelligence and Godhead that the mediation and atonement of Jesus Christ is instituted; and that noble being, man . . . is rendered capable of becoming a God, possessing the power, the majesty, the exaltation and the position of a God" (*Mediation and Atonement*, 140–41).

To Know God

Joseph Smith

Here, then, is eternal life—to know the only wise and true God; and you have got to learn how to be Gods yourselves, and to be kings and priests to God, the same as all Gods have done before you, namely, by going from one small degree to another, and from a small capacity to a great one; from grace to grace, from exaltation to exaltation, until you attain to the resurrection of the dead, and are able to dwell in everlasting burnings, and to sit in glory, as do those who sit enthroned in everlasting power. . . .

. . . How consoling . . . to know that, although the earthly tabernacle is laid down and dissolved, [our loved ones] shall rise again to dwell in everlasting burnings in immortal glory, not to sorrow, suffer, or die anymore; but they shall be heirs of God and joint heirs with Jesus Christ. What is it? To inherit the same power, the same glory and the same exaltation, until you arrive at the station of a God, and ascend the throne of eternal power, the same as those who have gone before. . . .

When you climb up a ladder, you must begin at the bottom and ascend step by step, until you arrive at the top; and so it is with the principles of the gospel—you must begin with the first and go on until you learn all the principles of exaltation. But it will be a great while after you have passed through the veil before you will have learned them. It is not all to be comprehended in this world; it will be a great work to learn our salvation and exaltation even beyond the grave.

Sources

Our Beginnings in Glory

"'Go and Be Faithful'" by John Taylor, from "The Mormon," 29 August 1857, in *Latter-day Prophets Speak: Selections from the Sermons and Writings of Church Presidents*, edited by Daniel H. Ludlow (Salt Lake City: Bookcraft, 1948), 8–9.

"Spirit Children of God" by Bruce R. McConkie, from *A New Witness for the Articles of Faith* (Salt Lake City: Deseret Book Co., 1985), 45.

"Immortal, Individual Spirits" by Robert J. Matthews, from *Selected Writings of Robert J. Matthews* (Salt Lake City: Deseret Book Co., 1999), 465–66.

"Chosen by the Divine" by Truman G. Madsen, from *Eternal Man* (Salt Lake City: Deseret Book Co., 1966), 39–40.

"The Spark of Awakened Memories" by Joseph F. Smith, from *Gospel Doctrine: Selections from the Sermons and Writings of Joseph F. Smith*, compiled by John A. Widtsoe (Salt Lake City: Deseret Book Co., 1939), 12–14.

"Free to Choose" by Joseph Fielding Smith, from "Is Man Immortal?" *Improvement Era* 19 (February 1916): 318–19, 321.

"Essential to Our Progression" by Bruce R. McConkie, from *The Mortal Messiah: From Bethlehem to Calvary*, 4 vols. (Salt Lake City: Deseret Book Co., 1979–81), 1:22–23.

"On Earth and in Heaven" by Brent L. Top, from *The Life Before* (Salt Lake City: Bookcraft, 1988), 92–94.

"'We Were There'" by Sheri Dew, from *No Doubt About It* (Salt Lake City: Deseret Book Co., 2001), 38–40.

"Satan's So-Called Shortcut to Salvation" by Robert J. Matthews, from *Selected Writings of Robert J. Matthews* (Salt Lake City: Deseret Book Co., 1999), 484–85.

"The Ultimate Act of Love" by Richard Eyre, from *Life Before Life* (Salt Lake City: Shadow Mountain, 2000), 104–6.

Falling to Mortality

"A Step Downward, yet Forward" by Orson F. Whitney, from "Significance of the Fall," *Improvement Era* 19 (March 1916): 402–3.

"The Gift of Death, the Gift of Life" by Bruce R. McConkie, from "Christ and the Creation," *Ensign*, June 1982, 9.

"Living by the Law of Obedience" by Hugh Nibley, from *Nibley on the Timely and the Timeless* (Provo: BYU Religious Studies Center, 1978), 280–81.

"The Problem and the Solution" by Stephen E. Robinson, from *Following Christ: The Parable of the Divers and More Good News* (Salt Lake City: Deseret Book Co., 1995), 43–45.

"Reinstated to the Royal Family" by Robert L. Millet, from *Alive in Christ: The Miracle of Spiritual Rebirth* (Salt Lake City: Deseret Book Co., 1997), 75–76.

"The Thorn and the Rose" by Orson F. Whitney, from "Blessings from the Tragedies of Life," *Improvement Era* 19 (January 1916): 200–201.

"Choose Wisely" by Stephen E. Robinson, from *Following Christ: The Parable of the Divers and More Good News* (Salt Lake City: Deseret Book Co., 1995), 47.

"Our Day to Do Our Best" by Ezra Taft Benson, from "Jesus Christ—Gifts and Expectations," *Ensign*, December 1988, 6.

"To Finish Is to Win" by Anne Osborn Poelman, from "Balance: The Joy of Perspective," in *LDS Women's Treasury: Insights and Inspiration for Today's Woman*, edited by Jay A. Parry (Salt Lake City: Deseret Book Co., 1997), 112–15, 117.

"Cultivating Heaven within Us" by George Q. Cannon, from *Gospel*

Truth: Discourses and Writings of President George Q. Cannon, edited by Jerreld L. Newquist (Salt Lake City: Deseret Book Co., 1987), 13.

"Selling the Summer Home in Babylon" by Sharon G. Larsen, from "Agency—A Blessing and a Burden," *Ensign*, November 1999, 11–13.

"The Bread of Adversity" by Truman G. Madsen, from *Four Essays on Love* (Salt Lake City: Bookcraft, 1971), 69–71.

"Sometimes He Will Not" by Spencer W. Kimball, from *Tragedy or Destiny?* (Salt Lake City: Deseret Book Co., 1977), 2–3.

"The Plan and the Work" by Hugh Nibley, from *Temple and Cosmos: Beyond This Ignorant Present*, edited by Don E. Norton (Salt Lake City and Provo: Deseret Book Co. and Foundation for Ancient Research and Mormon Studies, 1992), 555–56.

"Saviors on Mount Zion" by John A. Widtsoe, from *Utah Genealogical and Historical Magazine*, October 1934, 289.

"Following the Lord's Perfect Formula" by Mark E. Petersen, from "Eternal Togetherness," *Ensign*, November 1974, 48–49, 51.

"The Greatest Hope" by Anita R. Canfield, adapted from *A Perfect Brightness of Hope* (Salt Lake City: Deseret Book Co., 1991), 11–12.

Priorities, Perspectives, and Promises

"Unlocking Our Memories" by Truman G. Madsen, from *The Highest in Us* (Salt Lake City: Deseret Book Co., 1978), 17–18, 20–21.

"The Promise of Forever" by Spencer W. Kimball, from "An Eternal Hope in Christ," *Ensign*, November 1978, 71–72.

"Crossing the Chasm" by Cheryl Brown Mitchell, from "Complexities, Covenants, and Christ" in *To Rejoice As Women: Talks from the 1994 Women's Conference*, edited by Susette Fletcher Green and Dawn Hall Anderson (Salt Lake City: Deseret Book Co., 1995), 148–50.

"The Second Act" by Ardeth G. Kapp, from *My Neighbor, My Sister, My Friend* (Salt Lake City: Deseret Book Co., 1990), 4–5, 7.

"The Test, the Task, the Commandment" by Ezra Taft Benson, from *The Teachings of Ezra Taft Benson* (Salt Lake City: Bookcraft, 1988), 348–50.

"'Preparation for Joys Eternal'" by Parley P. Pratt, from *Key to the Science of Theology* (Salt Lake City: Deseret Book Co., 1978), 162–64.

"'Let the World Go'" by Sheri Dew, from "We Are Women of God," *Ensign*, November 1999, 97–98.

"To Behold the Face of God" by Hugh Nibley, from *The World and the Prophets*, 3d ed. (Salt Lake City and Provo: Deseret Book Co. and Foundation for Ancient Research and Mormon Studies, 1987), 264–67.

"The Road to Joy" by Hugh B. Brown, from *Continuing the Quest* (Salt Lake City: Deseret Book Co., 1961), 345–46.

"God's First Question" by Richard Eyre, from *Life Before Life* (Salt Lake City: Shadow Mountain, 2000), 139–41.

"Consecrate the Everyday" by Joan B. MacDonald, from *The Holiness of Everyday Life* (Salt Lake City: Deseret Book Co., 1995), 135–38.

"Eternal Life Is Now" by Mary B. Kirk, adapted from "Finding Holiness in Everyday Life," in *Clothed with Charity: Talks from the 1996 Women's Conference*, edited by Dawn Hall Anderson, Susette Fletcher Green, and Dlora Hall Dalton (Salt Lake City: Deseret Book Co., 1997), 116–17.

"All the Way Home" by Elaine L. Jack, from "Walk with Me," *Ensign*, May 1994, 15–16.

"A Light in the Storm" by Margaret D. Nadauld, from "Follow the Light," *Ensign*, May 1999, 94.

"Remember What We Forgot" by Ardeth G. Kapp, from *Rejoice! His Promises Are Sure* (Salt Lake City: Deseret Book Co., 1997), 81–83, 85–87.

"A God in Embryo" by John Taylor, from *The Gospel Kingdom: Selections from the Writings and Discourses of John Taylor,* edited by G. Homer Durham (Salt Lake City: Improvement Era, 1941), 52, 54–55.

The Doorway of Death

"A Blessing in Disguise" by Spencer W. Kimball, from *Tragedy or Destiny?* (Salt Lake City: Deseret Book Co., 1977), 6, 8–9, 12.

"From Birth to Death to Eternal Life" by Robert L. Millet and Joseph Fielding McConkie, from *The Life Beyond* (Salt Lake City: Bookcraft, 1986), 14–15.

"A Return Home" by Orson F. Whitney, from "We Walk by Faith," *Improvement Era* 19 (May 1916): 608–9.

"'Where Is Thy Sting?'" by George Q. Cannon, from *Gospel Truth: Discourses and Writings of President George Q. Cannon,* edited by Jerreld L. Newquist (Salt Lake City: Deseret Book Co., 1987), 61.

"An Absolute Guarantee" by Bruce R. McConkie, from "The Dead Who Die in the Lord," *Ensign,* November 1976, 107.

"Jesus' Example" by Spencer W. Kimball, from *The Teachings of Spencer W. Kimball,* edited by Edward L. Kimball (Salt Lake City: Bookcraft, 1982), 44–45.

"A Link in a Living Chain" by George Q. Cannon, from *Gospel Truth: Discourses and Writings of President George Q. Cannon,* edited by Jerrold L. Newquist (Salt Lake City: Deseret Book Co., 1987), 59–60.

"The State of the Soul" by Joseph F. Smith, from *Gospel Doctrine: Selections from the Sermons and Writings of Joseph F. Smith,* compiled by John A. Widtsoe (Salt Lake City: Deseret Book Co., 1939), 440–41.

"To Exist Eternally" by Brigham Young, from *Journal of Discourses,* 26 vols. (London: Latter-day Saints' Book Depot, 1854–86), 5:53–54.

"An Actual Death, a Literal Resurrection" by James E. Talmage, from *Articles of Faith* (Salt Lake City: Deseret Book Co., 1981), 344–46.

"'When the Voice Calls for the Dead'" by Joseph Smith, from *Teachings of the Prophet Joseph Smith,* edited by Joseph Fielding Smith (Salt Lake City: Deseret Book Co., 1976), 295–96.

"All Will Be Resurrected" by J. Reuben Clark Jr., from *On the Way to Immortality and Eternal Life* (Salt Lake City: Deseret Book Co., 1949), 147–50, 154–55.

"An Eternal Identity" by Joseph F. Smith, from Conference Report, April 1912, 135–37.

An Eternity of Glory

"His Work and His Glory" by Stephen E. Robinson, from *Following Christ: The Parable of the Divers and More Good News* (Salt Lake City: Deseret Book Co., 1995), 142–43.

"'How Will You Spend Eternity?'" by Orson F. Whitney, from Conference Report, October 1928, 63–65.

"Eternal Life Is God's Life" by Bruce R. McConkie, from *A New Witness for the Articles of Faith* (Salt Lake City: Deseret Book Co., 1985), 152–54.

"What Would You Give?" by Mark E. Petersen, from "What Will a Man Give?" *Ensign,* January 1974, 111.

"Unequaled Blessings" by Brigham Young, from *Journal of Discourses,* 26 vols. (London: Latter-day Saints' Book Depot, 1854–86), 8:63.

"Claim Your Crown" by Spencer W. Kimball, from "Kings and Priests" in *BYU Speeches of the Year,* 15 February 1966, 17–18.

"The Lord's Invitation" by Lorenzo Snow, from *Journal of Discourses,* 26 vols. (London: Latter-day Saints' Book Depot, 1854–86), 5:313–14.

"Blessed Are God's Children" by LeGrand Richards, from "What After Death?" *Ensign,* November 1974, 52.

"'Formed for Eternity'" by Joseph F. Smith, from *Gospel Doctrine: Selections from the Sermons and Writings of Joseph F. Smith,* compiled by John A. Widtsoe (Salt Lake City: Deseret Book Co., 1939), 277–78.

"Thirty-Five Million Years" by LeGrand Richards, from "Be Ye Prepared," *Ensign*, November 1981, 28.

"'Adapted to the Highest Glories'" by Parley P. Pratt, from *Key to the Science of Theology* (Salt Lake City: Deseret Book Co., 1978), 62–67.

"The Emperor's Child" by Lorenzo Snow, from *The Teachings of Lorenzo Snow*, edited by Clyde J. Williams (Salt Lake City: Bookcraft, 1984), 2–3.

"Joint Heirs with Christ" by Robert L. Millet, from *Alive in Christ: The Miracle of Spiritual Rebirth* (Salt Lake City: Deseret Book Co., 1997), 79–81.

"The Spark of Divinity" by George Q. Cannon, from *Gospel Truth: Discourses and Writings of President George Q. Cannon*, edited by Jerreld L. Newquist (Salt Lake City: Deseret Book Co., 1987), 86–87.

"Something of God in Us" by Hugh B. Brown, from *Continuing the Quest* (Salt Lake City: Deseret Book Co., 1961), 31–32.

"A Heavenly Mandate" by Tad R. Callister, from *The Infinite Atonement* (Salt Lake City: Deseret Book Co., 2000), 232–33.

"The Purpose for Our Creation" by Brigham Young, from *Journal of Discourses*, 26 vols. (London: Latter-day Saints' Book Depot, 1854–86), 3:93.

"'Drink the Heavenly Draught, and Live'" by Robert L. Millet and Joseph Fielding McConkie, from *The Life Beyond* (Salt Lake City: Bookcraft, 1986), 143, 152–53.

"'Sit with Me in My Throne'" by Tad R. Callister, from *The Infinite Atonement* (Salt Lake City: Deseret Book Co., 2000), 244–45.

"To Know God" by Joseph Smith, from *Teachings of the Prophet Joseph Smith*, edited by Joseph Fielding Smith (Salt Lake City: Deseret Book Co., 1976), 346–48.